The Bride and Groom's First Cookbook

Doubleday

NEW YORK LONDON TORONTO

SYDNEY AUCKLAND

The Bride and Groom's First Cookbook

ABIGAIL KIRSCH

WITH SUSAN M. GREENBERG

TO ALL THE BRIDES AND GROOMS WHO MADE THIS COOKBOOK FUN TO WRITE

BY ASKING FOR EASY, TIMESAVING DELICIOUS RECIPES

Published by Doubleday

a division of Bantam Doubleday Dell Publishing Group, Inc.

1540 Broadway, New York, New York 10036

DOUBLEDAY and the portrayal of an anchor with a dolphin are trademarks of Doubleday,
a division of Bantam Doubleday Dell Publishing Group, Inc.

Book Design by Gretchen Achilles

Illustrations copyright © 1996 by Stephanie Langley

Library of Congress Cataloging-in-Publication Data
Kirsch, Abigail.
The bride and groom's first cookbook / Abigail Kirsch and Susan M.
Greenberg. — 1st ed.
p. cm.
Includes index.
1. Dinners and dining. 2. Entertaining. 3. Cookery for two.
4. Menus I. Greenberg, Susan M. II. Title.
TX737.K57 1996
642—dc20   95-18377
CIP

ISBN 0-385-47635-3

Printed in the United States of America

February 1996
3 5 7 9 10 8 6 4 2

Acknowledgments

Our special thanks to Pam Bernstein, our literary agent, Judith Kern, our editor at Doubleday, and Alison Awerbuch, the executive chef at Tappan Hill. We also want to acknowledge the culinary expertise of Elizabeth Bourne, Anita Carson, Nancy Donato, Cecelia Giunta, Pat Guardino, Anna Hogan, Geraldine Lasala, Janet MacEachen, Ralph MacEachen, Janice Murphy, Megan Neisser, Michelle Orpaz, Amy Post, John Reilly, Scott Robbins, Ed Steinberg, and Mary Wiltshire. Thanks also to Rhoda Beningson and Jody Murphy.

Contents

CHAPTER 10
GLOSSARY OF COOKING TERMS   289

CHAPTER 11
THE WELL-STOCKED PANTRY   293

CHAPTER 12
REGISTRY PLANNER   301

INDEX   305

Introduction

Cooking is fun. Cooking together can be funny, entertaining, poignant, challenging, and fulfilling. Too many cooks may spoil the broth but two palates in the kitchen can produce an endless array of delicious dinners. The trick is to make the experience easy, affordable, and nonstressful. To ensure that your cooking experience is as pleasurable as possible, Sue and I have suggested both preparation and cooking times for the recipes, including timesaving "Do-Ahead" tips. We've listed the cookware required, cooked with obtainable ingredients, and honored your budget with full understanding of your hectic schedules.

Don't be intimidated! Imagine we're in the kitchen cooking along with you. Say to yourself, "What would Abigail do in this situation?" While preparing the following recipes, we've thought about for whom you are cooking—yourselves, parents, friends, business associates—and where you may run into trouble. Everyone does and it's okay! Cooking is a learning experience. In "sidebars," we've tried to anticipate problems and to suggest simple solutions. And finally, we've noted that using expensive ingredients and table decor is not a prerequisite to a successful meal. Be imaginative and you're sure to succeed.

In the menu section of the book, we've divided meals into three categories. The dollar signs will be your guide to determining which menu best fits your food allowance.

- ❖   The single dollar sign, $, indicates an inexpensive meal.

- ❖ $$ indicates a moderate meal.

- ❖ $$$ indicates an expensive meal.

Please remember that prices vary in different regions of the country and you'll have spirits, wine, and table decor to consider.

Our philosophy of food has always centered around simple and honest cuisine. Perhaps one of the most satisfying meals we have ever eaten was a lunch in the Napa Valley—a sandwich of grilled chicken, sliced avocado, and roasted red peppers nestled in grilled pita bread. The individual tastes of the chicken, avocado, and pepper were distinct, yet served together, they created a whole new eating experience. If you always begin by buying the freshest ingredients, your recipes are guaranteed to succeed. Experiment, substitute seasonal items as available, and you will enjoy the pure taste of dazzling food, whatever the occasion.

As the founder/chef of Abigail Kirsch at Tappan Hill, an elegant mansion overlooking the Hudson River, I've met with thousands of brides and grooms to discuss their likes and dislikes and to create menus tailored to their individual tastes. As a result, I've come to understand what newlyweds need and want. Some brides literally want a spotlight on them, while others don't even want a cake-cutting ceremony. As I say to all the brides and grooms at Tappan Hill, "Here is an outline of a menu, now design yours. Put the 'you' in it."

So it is with the foods you prepare. Read the recipes in the front section and menu-plan together. Combine the recipes to make an interesting meal. Many of the recipes have "serve with" suggestions. Tailor your meals to your tastes and those of your guests. Your objective is to provide a comfortable atmosphere for your guests and yourselves and to recognize individual dietary concerns: vegetarian, low-fat diet, allergy to shellfish.

The most important ingredient in planning *your first* dinner party is a sense of humor! It goes a long way toward easing a serious case of anxiety. The angst before my first party was alleviated when Tony, the butcher, gave me his secret recipe for sliced steak with mushroom sauce, along with a very good cut of beef. Tony became my cooking guru, and my guests had the dubious pleasure of dining on the same menu for at least one year.

As newlyweds, Bob and I did our entertaining on Saturday nights. We would run a mini-marathon all evening. I always set the table the night before (and still do). Bob bought the wine and the flowers, lit the candles, and arranged the place cards. I cooked dinner. As our guests finished each course, the dishes were promptly cleared and stacked in the dishwasher, allowing us leisurely time after dinner for socializing. Our goal: no dirty dishes after the guests left.

Bob and I often had dinner guests and soon discovered that one-dish recipes served with great salads and hearty breads were a nonstressful way to entertain. Because many of the dishes could be cooked in advance, the trauma of wondering "is this recipe going to work for me" was laid to rest. My so-called good friends never let me forget burning my grandmother's secret recipe for cabbage soup. This culinary calamity could have been avoided if I had had the foresight to try the recipe in advance. Then, too, I would have realized the need for a heavy-duty soup pot in our kitchen registry. The soup was cooked in the only big pot I could find . . . a thin washtub. The soup burned, and with a very red face, I served salad and bread for dinner! That taught me to simmer soup in a heavy-bottomed pot. I also learned the first step to a successful dinner party: *Read the recipes from beginning to end and gather all your necessary ingredients, utensils, and cookware before you begin.*

Register! Register! Register!

Register, register, register! When the honeymoon is over and you begin your domestic life together, you will want to open your cabinets and see *your* favorite china, crystal, and silver. You will want your kitchen stocked with *your* favorite appliances and gadgets. Don't leave anything to chance. Make your wishes known *before* all those wedding guests go shopping for gifts. There's nothing like receiving a nest of orange mixing bowls when your kitchen is red and white (of course, Aunt Em bought them at an outlet store in Kansas and you can't return or exchange them)!

Bridal registries were created for the convenience of both the guests and the bride and groom. Guests can call or visit a store and find a gift within their price range, knowing it will be welcomed and appreciated by the newlyweds.

Only a generation ago, the words "Bridal Registry" evoked images of fine china, crystal, and silver displayed in stores such as Tiffany & Co., Shreve Crump & Low, Gump's, Neiman-Marcus, and the like. Added to these were discounters such as Michael Fina, Fortunoff, and Ross-Simons. Today there are registries in a wide range of stores. Traditional fine china shops and department stores have been joined by hardware stores, bed and bath shops, sporting goods stores, travel agents, music stores, and even banks anxious to help gift-givers make their selections count.

Williams-Sonoma; Crate & Barrel; and Bed Bath & Beyond have a veritable network of stores across the country. Computers make the registering process extremely simple. Orders can be faxed as well as telephoned in on 800 toll-free numbers. Thus, a relative in California can send a bride and groom the cabbage soup tureen and matching bowls they registered for in Buffalo. A couple in Vermont will be delighted to receive the matching backpacks and double sleeping bag they registered for at a national sporting goods store!

Today's couples register as soon as they're engaged. Since friends, family, and co-workers often give showers, early registering assures that couples will receive the gifts of their choice. Among the many unique registry items these days are cookie jars, pasta makers, knife blocks, shower curtains, and fondue sets. A recipe box makes a welcome shower gift. Each invited guest is asked to bring his or her favorite recipe on a three-by-five-inch index card. The filled box is then given to the bride and groom. For an extra touch, have the recipe cards printed with "From the Kitchen of" and the bride and groom's names. (Find out if the bride is changing her last name, hyphenating it, or keeping her maiden name!) Include a printed recipe card in each shower invitation.

Finally, in Chapter 12, we've included a list of kitchen essentials you'll want to make certain to include on your registry.

Wedding Lore and Customs

The celebration of marriage has been surrounded by ceremony, ritual, and pomp since the beginning of recorded history. Although photography was yet to be developed, brides and grooms in the ancient world found their own methods of recording the most important day in their lives. The ancient Greeks captured the ceremony in beautiful pictures painted on vases. Later, oils, watercolors, etchings, and pen-and-ink drawings were used to create mementos and, incidentally, to provide insight for future historians. From these artistic renderings, we've learned a great deal about how our ancestors celebrated the ritual of marriage. Today's wedding album will serve the same purpose for future generations.

In almost every society until the twentieth century, marriages were arranged. (This practice still exists in certain parts of the world.) Marriage first, love later; the word "romance" was never used. The concept of arranged marriages obviously worked well since divorces were easy to obtain, yet the divorce rate was far lower than it is today.

Most marriage contracts were looked upon as commercial transactions, usually made between two families without the consent of either the bride or the groom. Depending on the local custom, marriages took place in the home or public squares, with the bride and groom often meeting for the first time. While many of today's weddings are religious in nature and take place in churches or synagogues, many brides and grooms are quite creative in their choice of locale. Weddings are held on mountaintops, in hot-air balloons, under water, and at sporting events. One couple exchanged vows at halftime on the football field at the Yale Bowl! They had met as undergraduates while playing in the marching band. What more appropriate place to hold their ceremony than on the field during halftime, while the band played on!

The custom of having bridesmaids and ushers, or groomsmen, in the wedding party has its origins in the pagan ritual of marriage by "capture." If a clan did not have enough women available for its eligible bachelors, its young men raided neighboring tribes and captured their women. Some of the captures were friendly, while others were quite militant. Bridesmaids and groomsmen played very important roles in these societies. Groomsmen served as comrades-in-arms, helping their friends capture wives! Bridesmaids dressed in the same clothes as the bride, confusing the groom and his men, thus enabling the bride to elude capture! Bridesmaids and groomsmen are still an integral part of today's weddings, but happily, in modern times their roles have become supportive rather than protective.

The wedding ring also has its origin in pagan times. According to the ancient Greeks, Prometheus made the first wedding band out of smelted metal for strength and endurance. The unbroken circle was believed to signify the harmony of marriage. In the Old Testament, Adam presented Cain with a ring of iron to give to his wife as a symbol of unity. Today, precious metals—silver and gold—have replaced the original ring of iron. Modern-day adaptations of the many pagan rites have become big business! Photographers, jewelers, musicians, and florists have all prospered from ancient customs.

Flowers have always been synonymous with weddings. In Europe, a garland of orange blossoms, symbolizing virginity or innocence as well as fertility, was often used as a headpiece for the bride. This custom was brought to the United States by the earliest settlers. Today flowers are usually selected to match the bridesmaids' dresses or the decor at the wedding reception!

In ancient Rome, grooms used a torch to light the first fire in their new homes and then tossed the torch to the waiting wedding party. Since this practice had dangerous side effects, an enterprising flower merchant came up with the idea of replacing the torch with a bouquet of flowers! It was the French who added the superstition that whoever caught the bouquet would be the next to marry.

Food has always played a major role in wedding festivities. The ritualistic breaking of bread provides a commonality among world cultures differing in many other aspects. The Greeks ate cake for a sweet and fruitful life, while in Rome the bride and groom consecrated their marriage by eating a special cake dedicated to Jupiter. Rice cakes were—and still are—symbols of good fortune in Asia. The simple eating of a rice cake in Japan indicated the completion of the marriage ceremony in earlier times. To indicate the importance of food, it is interesting to note that Eskimo women have no dowry, only a cooking pot!

The shattering of a glass is another custom practiced in many cultures. In pagan times, crockery was smashed to ward off evil spirits. Today, Jewish grooms break a glass to symbolize the destruction of the First Temple. Even during life's happiest moments, the unfortunate must be remembered.

The customs and rituals surrounding weddings are many. They've evolved throughout history in every society and religious group. Pagan superstitions are intertwined with both civil and religious traditions. Some of the oldest wedding customs have survived despite state and/or religious intervention. If Alexander the Great, Julius Caesar, or Confucius could attend a wedding today, he would probably witness familiar rituals!

Before You Start Cooking

With the exception of the recipes in the chapters on "Hors d'Oeuvre," "Breads," and "Desserts," all our recipes are written to yield four servings.

In most instances, however, you'll want leftovers. Our **Cook's Tips** give you a variety of ways to use leftovers. Or—simply freeze half and have a complete meal at your fingertips after a long day when neither of you has the time (or energy) to cook.

Follow these eleven tips for a successful cooking experience:

1. Read the recipes from beginning to end and gather all the necessary ingredients, utensils, and cookware before you begin.

2. Check your pantry and refrigerator for ingredients on hand. With a well-stocked pantry, you'll be amazed at how little you'll have to buy.

3. Make certain your knives are razor sharp.

4. Don't forget to wear aprons.

5. Work over waxed paper or paper toweling to make clean-up as quick and easy as possible.

6. Always have a slightly damp towel nearby to wipe up spills on counters and range tops as they happen.

7. Clean and put away cookware and utensils as soon as you are finished using them.

8. Have your oven calibrated by a professional once a year.

9. Remember to preheat the oven when indicated in a recipe. A preheated oven should wait for you instead of you waiting for it.

10. Dried herbs are more pungent than fresh ones. Use one third to one half the amount of a fresh herb.

11. After freezing any prepared food, always reseason to taste before serving.

Chapter 1

Hors d'Oeuvre

HORS D'OEUVRE SHOULD PLEASE THE EYE AND TITILLATE THE PALATE. THEY SHOULD TEMPT THE APPETITE, NOT SATISFY IT. FOR A WELL-ROUNDED MENU, CONSIDER APPETIZERS THAT COMPLEMENT THE REST OF YOUR MEAL. IF THE MAIN COURSE CONTAINS SHRIMP, DON'T SERVE A SHELLFISH HORS D'OEUVRE. IF MEAT IS THE ENTRÉE, SAVE A MEATBALL HORS D'OEUVRE FOR ANOTHER MENU.

OUR HORS D'OEUVRE RECIPES ARE FOR TWELVE SERVINGS. HALVE OR DOUBLE THE RECIPES ACCORDING TO YOUR NEEDS.

AN ENTIRE COCKTAIL PARTY MENU CAN BE CREATED FROM THE RECIPES IN THIS SECTION. WE TAKE THREE APPROACHES TO COCKTAILS AND HORS D'OEUVRE. THE FIRST, AND OUR FAVORITE, IS AN INTIMATE SIT-DOWN PARTY FOR TWO TO SIX OF OUR NEAREST AND DEAREST FRIENDS. FOR THIS SMALL, FAMILIAR PARTY, FOOD IS A VERY IMPORTANT FOCAL POINT. YOU ALL SIT IN COMFORT AND CHAT TOGETHER WHILE CONSTANTLY REACHING FOR MUNCHIES. THE MENU FOR THIS SMALL GATHERING CAN BE DESIGNED WITH PLATES AND FORKS IN MIND, SINCE EVERYONE IS COMFORTABLY SEATED.

THEN THERE IS THE GATHERING OF A DOZEN OR SO FRIENDS THAT MAY OCCUR AFTER SKIING, HIKING, SAILING, OR A TRIP TO THE BEACH. THERE IS SOCIAL MOVEMENT AT THIS PARTY, WITH SOME OF THE GUESTS STANDING AND THE REST SITTING. GUESTS ARE BUSY NETWORKING, SHARING EXPERIENCES, AND, PERHAPS, ARE NOT AS ATTUNED TO THE FOOD. THE DOZEN OR SO FRIENDS YOU ENTERTAIN SHOULD BE SERVED "PICK-UP" FOOD SINCE THE PARTY HAS NOW GROWN AND SPACE CAN BE LIMITED.

FINALLY, THERE IS THE GRAND "PAY-BACK" PARTY FOR A CROWD OF FIFTY OR MORE. IN THIS SCENARIO, MANY PEOPLE ARE CRAMMED INTO YOUR HOME AND IMBIBING. THEY ARE SO BUSY SOCIALIZING THAT THEY MAY FORGET ABOUT EATING. YOUR LARGEST PARTY REQUIRES WHAT WE FONDLY LABEL, "HORS D'OEUVRE BY THE BITE" . . . FOOD YOU CAN EASILY PICK UP AND POP IN YOUR MOUTH.

TO MASTER THE ART OF BEING A GUEST AND ENJOYING YOUR OWN PARTY, FOLLOW OUR SUGGESTED TIMETABLES. YOU WILL DISCOVER THAT MANY OF THE HORS D'OEUVRE CAN BE FROZEN AND THAT VIRTUALLY ALL OF THEM CAN BE PLACED AROUND YOUR HOME BEFORE THE FIRST GUESTS ARRIVE.

Cilantro Toast Crisps

❧

KITCHENWARE: serrated bread knife, chef's knife, small stainless-steel saucepan, pastry brush, pepper mill, baking sheet

PREPARATION TIME: 10 minutes

BAKING TIME: 4 minutes

DO-AHEAD: Make the oil, garlic, and cilantro mixture up to 2 days ahead and refrigerate, covered. Reheat the oil before brushing on the bread.

1/2 CUP VIRGIN OLIVE OIL

2 CLOVES GARLIC, MINCED

2 TABLESPOONS FINELY CHOPPED FRESH CILANTRO

1 BAGUETTE-STYLE FRENCH BREAD, CUT INTO 1/4-INCH SLICES

FRESHLY GROUND PEPPER

1. Preheat the oven to 425 degrees.

2. Put the olive oil, garlic, and cilantro in the saucepan and heat until warm.

3. Brush each piece of bread with the spiced oil. Reach down to the bottom of the pan with the brush to make sure that the spices are evenly distributed on each slice of bread.

4. Sprinkle the crisps with pepper, arrange on the baking sheet, and bake for 4 minutes, until golden brown.

12 SERVINGS

COOK'S TIPS:

❖ Flavored oils can be prepared in advance. It is best to cover the oils and store them in the refrigerator to maintain their freshness. The chill in the refrigerator may make the oil cloudy. Don't worry! Just bring it to room temperature and the haze will disappear.

❖ These savory crisps are excellent with grilled or sautéed beef.

❖ Spread the crisps with black beans or soft cheese (Brie or Explorateur) for a quick snack.

Garlic-Scented Gouda Cheese with Caraway Seeds

WITH GRANDMOTHERS WHO DELIGHTED IN FEEDING US THICK SLICES OF PUMPERNICKEL BREAD

SLATHERED WITH BUTTER AND FRESH GARLIC, IT'S NO SURPRISE THAT GARLIC HAS

ALWAYS BEEN ONE OF OUR FAVORITES. THIS RECIPE IS A WONDERFUL WAY

TO SATISFY THAT YEN FOR GARLIC.

KITCHENWARE: serrated knife, chef's knife, food processor

PREPARATION TIME: 20 minutes

DO-AHEAD: Make the cheese mixture the day before, cover, and refrigerate. Bring the cheese to room temperature before filling the bread.

14 OUNCES GOUDA CHEESE

1/2 CUP BEER

1 TEASPOON DIJON MUSTARD

1/8 TEASPOON GRATED NUTMEG

4 TABLESPOONS (1/2 STICK) SWEET
BUTTER, SOFTENED

2 CLOVES GARLIC, PEELED

4 OUNCES CREAM CHEESE, SOFTENED

1 ROUND PUMPERNICKEL BREAD (ABOUT 8
INCHES IN DIAMETER)

1 TABLESPOON CARAWAY SEEDS

1. Remove the wax covering from the cheese and cut the cheese into small pieces.

2. Put the cheese, beer, mustard, nutmeg, butter, garlic, and cream cheese in the bowl of the food processor. Process for 50 seconds, or until the ingredients form a ball. The consistency will be creamy.

   Don't panic; the cheese may remain a little lumpy after processing.

3. Hollow out a 3-inch circle in the center of the bread. Spoon the cheese into the bread and sprinkle it with caraway seeds.

SERVICE: If there isn't time to prepare the bread, serve the cheese in a bowl or crock surrounded by crackers or tortilla chips.

COOK'S TIPS:

- ❖   The cheese is delicious served on croustades with a green salad.

- ❖   For a great sandwich, use the spread under smoked ham or turkey.

- ❖   The tangy taste of cheese makes a perfect dip for crisp raw vegetables.

Seviche of Shrimp

SHRIMP SEVICHE IS A LITTLE TWIST ON A RECIPE THAT IS TRADITIONALLY MADE WITH
SCALLOPS. THE BITING CITRUS IN THE LIME CREATES A WONDERFUL FRESH FLAVOR
AND ACCENTS THE CRUNCHINESS OF THE SHRIMP.

KITCHENWARE: chef's knife, whisk, pepper mill, rubber gloves (see Cook's Tips), stainless-steel medium saucepan, large plastic bowl with fitted lid

PREPARATION TIME: 30 minutes

MARINATING TIME: 6 to 8 hours

COOKING TIME: 3 minutes

DO-AHEAD: Make the marinade the day before and refrigerate. Reheat it before adding the shrimp in step 1.

2 TABLESPOONS LIME JUICE
(1 MEDIUM LIME)

2 TABLESPOONS VIRGIN OLIVE OIL

2 MEDIUM CLOVES GARLIC, MINCED

¼ TEASPOON SALT

½ TEASPOON FRESHLY GROUND PEPPER

3 SCALLIONS, THINLY SLICED
(GREEN STEM ONLY)

2 TEASPOONS MINCED JALAPEÑO PEPPER

2 POUNDS MEDIUM-SIZE RAW SHRIMP,
PEELED AND DEVEINED

1 TEASPOON DIJON MUSTARD

½ CUP SEEDED AND DICED TOMATOES

1 TABLESPOON CHOPPED FRESH CILANTRO

1. Put the lime juice, olive oil, garlic, salt, pepper, scallions, and jalapeño pepper in the saucepan. Bring to a simmer and cook for 2 minutes. Add the shrimp and cook for 1 minute more. Remove from the heat and whisk in the mustard.

   The shrimp will not cook through in 1 minute. Marinating the shrimp will do the final job for you.

2. Place the seviche in the plastic bowl and add the tomatoes and cilantro. Mix well. Cover with the fitted lid and refrigerate for 6 to 8 hours. Stir a few times to ensure the shrimp marinate evenly.

SERVICE: Serve the seviche in a decorative china or glass bowl with Cilantro Toast Crisps (page 11).

COOK'S TIPS:

❖ The inner skin of a jalapeño pepper causes irritation to the skin. When seeding and slicing the peppers, wear rubber gloves and keep your hands away from your eyes.

❖ Halibut, swordfish, tuna, or scallops are ideal substitutes for the shrimp.

❖ Serve the seviche as a first course over a bed of lettuce or piled high in an avocado or hollowed-out tomato.

Bruschetta Crisps

BRUSCHETTA IS ALWAYS A HIT. ADD IT TO BEACH PARTY, PICNIC, AND TAILGATE MENUS. SERVE IT WITH BOTH ROASTED GARLIC AND SHALLOTS (PAGE 18) AND BLACK OLIVE PESTO (PAGE 19) TO SATISFY A VARIETY OF TASTES.

KITCHENWARE: hand grater (see Cook's Tips), serrated bread knife, pastry brush, small stainless-steel saucepan, baking sheet

PREPARATION TIME: 5 minutes

BAKING TIME: 4 minutes

DO-AHEAD: Make the toast crisps in advance, wrap well, and store in the freezer. To serve, recrisp in a warm oven.

½ CUP VIRGIN OLIVE OIL

2 TABLESPOONS FINELY CHOPPED FRESH BASIL

2 BAGUETTE-STYLE FRENCH BREADS, CUT INTO ¼-INCH SLICES

½ CUP GRATED PARMESAN CHEESE

1. Preheat the oven to 425 degrees.

2. Warm the oil and basil in the saucepan. Brush each piece of bread with the oil and sprinkle with Parmesan cheese.

3. Arrange the bread on the baking sheet and bake for 4 minutes, until golden brown.

12 SERVINGS

SERVICE: Arrange the Bruschetta Crisps in a basket or on a silver tray lined with a napkin. Spoon the Roasted Garlic and Shallots and Black Olive Pesto toppings into small bowls with spreading knives. This is a "do-it-yourself" hors d'oeuvre.

COOK'S TIPS:

❖ We like to buy a large piece of fresh Parmesan cheese and grate it as needed for our recipes. Make sure to wrap it well in plastic wrap before storing in the refrigerator.

❖ Top bruschetta with sliced plum tomatoes, grilled eggplant, or diced smoked ham.

Roasted Garlic and Shallots

❦

KITCHENWARE: chef's knife, baking pan, aluminum foil

PREPARATION TIME: 20 minutes

COOKING TIME: 20 to 30 minutes

DO-AHEAD: The whole recipe can be made up to 2 days in advance. Refrigerate, covered, and warm before serving.

2 HEADS GARLIC, UNPEELED	**1 BAY LEAF**
4 LARGE SHALLOTS, UNPEELED	**2 TABLESPOONS VIRGIN OLIVE OIL**
2 SPRIGS ROSEMARY	

1. Preheat the oven to 350 degrees.

2. Separate the cloves of garlic. Place the garlic, shallots, rosemary, and bay leaf on the baking pan. Sprinkle with 1 tablespoon of the oil. Cover the baking pan tightly with foil. Bake for 20 to 30 minutes, until the garlic and shallots are very soft.

   Separating raw cloves from a head of garlic is easy. Simply press or bang the flat side of a chef's knife against the entire head.

3. Squeeze the roasted garlic and shallots out of their skins. Discard the rosemary and bay leaf. Add the remaining oil and mash the vegetables with a fork or the broad side of a chef's knife.

MAKES ½ CUP

SERVICE: Put the Roasted Garlic and Shallots in a small bowl and serve as a spread with Bruschetta Crisps (page 16).

COOK'S TIP: Garlic develops a sweet taste after roasting. Add it to mashed potatoes, turnips, or spaghetti squash for a subtle flavor.

Black Olive Pesto

KITCHENWARE: chef's knife, pepper mill, food processor

PREPARATION TIME: 15 minutes

DO-AHEAD: Make the pesto up to 2 days in advance. Be sure to cover the spread tightly and refrigerate.

3 CLOVES GARLIC, PEELED	**¹/₃ CUP PITTED NIÇOISE OLIVES**
2 ANCHOVY FILLETS	**1 ¹/₂ TEASPOONS VIRGIN OLIVE OIL**
1 TEASPOON PINE NUTS	**1 ¹/₂ TEASPOONS FRESH LEMON JUICE**
¹/₃ CUP PITTED BLACK OLIVES	**¹/₄ TEASPOON FRESHLY GROUND PEPPER**

1. Put the garlic, anchovies, pine nuts, and olives in the bowl of the food processor fitted with the cutting knife. Process until smooth.

2. Using the pulse button, slowly add the olive oil and lemon juice. Season with pepper.

MAKES 1 CUP

SERVICE: Put the Black Olive Pesto in a small bowl and serve as a spread with Bruschetta Crisps (page 16).

COOK'S TIPS:

❖ Try the pesto on grilled French bread.

❖ It also makes a wonderful dressing for grilled steak, seafood, or vegetables.

Apricot-Glazed Chicken Wings

THE COMBINATION OF INGREDIENTS MAKES THESE GLAZED CHICKEN WINGS
SIMPLY IRRESISTIBLE.

KITCHENWARE: fine grater, chef's knife, pepper mill, food processor, large stainless-steel bowl, baking sheet

PREPARATION TIME: 10 minutes

BAKING TIME: 25 minutes

DO-AHEAD: Make the glaze and add the chicken wings a day ahead. Cover and refrigerate. Bring to room temperature before baking.

1/2 CUP HONEY	1 TABLESPOON CHOPPED FRESH GINGER
1/2 CUP APRICOT PRESERVES	1/8 TEASPOON CAYENNE
2 TEASPOONS HOISIN SAUCE	2 TEASPOONS GRATED ORANGE ZEST
2 TEASPOONS SOY SAUCE	SALT AND FRESHLY GROUND BLACK PEPPER
3 TABLESPOONS BROWN SUGAR	
4 LARGE CLOVES GARLIC, PEELED	36 CHICKEN WINGS, TIPS REMOVED
	1/4 CUP SESAME SEEDS

1.   Preheat the oven to 350 degrees.

2.   Put the honey, apricot preserves, hoisin sauce, soy sauce, sugar, garlic, and ginger in the bowl of the food processor. Process until smooth. Add the cayenne and zest and pulse for 2 seconds. Pour the glaze into the stainless-steel bowl.

3.   Salt and pepper the chicken wings. Toss the wings in the glaze, coating well on all sides. Transfer the chicken to the baking sheet. Bake for 15 minutes, then increase the oven temperature to 450 degrees. Sprinkle the wings with the sesame seeds and continue to bake for 10 minutes more, until toasty brown. Cool to room temperature.

SERVICE: Serve at room temperature. Arrange the chicken wings in baskets or on oriental-style serving platters.

COOK'S TIPS:

❖   Provide moist towelettes for guests. While scrumptious, chicken wings are messy to eat.

❖   The wings can be served as a main course with a green salad and seasoned rice.

❖   Freeze the raw wing tips and use them to make Mom's Chicken Soup (page 44).

❖   Try the glaze on pork chops or chicken breasts.

Chili Meatballs with Zesty Tomato Sauce

THERE IS NOTHING LIKE HOT CHILI TO SATISFY RAVENOUS APPETITES ON A COLD, WINTRY DAY. THIS FIERY FOOD IS AN OLD-FASHIONED, "STICK-TO-YOUR-RIBS" HORS D'OEUVRE.

KITCHENWARE: chef's knife, pepper mill, large bowl, medium sauté pan, slotted spoon, paper toweling

PREPARATION TIME: 20 minutes (not including Zesty Tomato Sauce)

COOKING TIME: 20 minutes

DO-AHEAD: Mix and form the meatballs a day in advance. Cover tightly and refrigerate. Bring the raw meatballs to room temperature before cooking.

1 RECIPE ZESTY TOMATO SAUCE (RECIPE FOLLOWS)

1 MEDIUM ONION, FINELY CHOPPED

2 CLOVES GARLIC, FINELY CHOPPED

¼ CUP TOMATO SAUCE

2 TEASPOONS CHILI POWDER

½ TEASPOON CAYENNE

¼ TEASPOON GROUND CUMIN

SALT AND FRESHLY GROUND BLACK PEPPER

1½ POUNDS LEAN GROUND BEEF

¼ CUP VEGETABLE OIL

GARNISH:

1 TABLESPOON CHOPPED FRESH FLAT-LEAF PARSLEY

1.   Prepare the Zesty Tomato Sauce.

2.   While the sauce simmers, in a large bowl, combine the onion, garlic, tomato sauce, seasonings, and beef. Mix well. Form the beef into 1-inch balls. You should have about 24 meatballs.

3.   Heat the oil in the sauté pan. Sauté the meatballs until they are evenly browned on all sides.

Be sure the meatballs are not touching one another in the pan or they will steam instead of brown.

4. Remove the meatballs from the pan with a slotted spoon and drain on paper toweling.

5. Simmer them in the Zesty Tomato Sauce for 10 minutes.

12 SERVINGS

SERVICE: Ladle the meatballs and sauce into a shallow serving dish (about 2 inches deep). Sprinkle with chopped parsley. Serve at room temperature with toothpicks.

COOK'S TIPS:

❖ Leftover meatballs are terrific in a hero sandwich.

❖ Crumble cooked meatballs, top with grated Monterey Jack cheese, and serve with nachos.

❖ Zesty Tomato Sauce is perfect on meat loaf, deep-fried calamari, or barbecued shrimp.

ZESTY TOMATO SAUCE

KITCHENWARE: chef's knife, pepper mill, medium sauté pan

PREPARATION TIME: 10 minutes

COOKING TIME: 12 minutes

1 TABLESPOON VEGETABLE OIL

1 MEDIUM ONION, FINELY CHOPPED

2 CUPS BEEF BROTH (FRESH OR CANNED, UNSALTED)

1 CUP TOMATO SAUCE

2 TABLESPOONS TOMATO PASTE

$1/4$ CUP CHOPPED DRAINED MEDIUM/HOT CANNED GREEN CHILIES

$1/8$ TEASPOON CAYENNE

SALT AND FRESHLY GROUND BLACK PEPPER

Heat the oil in a sauté pan. Sauté the onion until translucent. Add the remaining sauce ingredients and simmer for 10 minutes.

MAKES 2$1/2$ CUPS

Swiss Fondue, Vegetables, Fruit, and French Bread

FONDUE IS FUN TO EAT, EASY TO PREPARE, AND A PERFECT ICE BREAKER

FOR GUESTS MEETING FOR THE FIRST TIME.

KITCHENWARE: small bowl, medium heavy saucepan, wooden spoon, chef's knife, vegetable peeler, food processor with grating blade (or cheese grater), fondue pot (or small chafer), skewers or fondue forks

PREPARATION TIME: 20 minutes

COOKING TIME: 6 minutes

DO-AHEAD: The day before, grate the cheeses and refrigerate, tightly covered. Also, prepare the vegetables and refrigerate, tightly covered. Don't cut the fruit ahead, or it will turn brown.

CHEESE:

1 TABLESPOON CORNSTARCH

2 TABLESPOONS CHERRY LIQUEUR

1 CLOVE GARLIC, PEELED AND HALVED

1 1/4 CUPS DRY WHITE WINE

3/4 POUND GRUYÈRE CHEESE, FINELY GRATED

3/4 POUND EMMENTALER CHEESE, FINELY GRATED

1 TABLESPOON DIJON MUSTARD

1/8 TEASPOON SALT

1/4 TEASPOON CAYENNE

1/8 TEASPOON GRATED NUTMEG

VEGETABLES, FRUIT, AND BREAD:

1 CAULIFLOWER, BROKEN INTO FLORETS

1 BUNCH BROCCOLI, BROKEN INTO FLORETS

4 CARROTS, PEELED, CUT INTO STICKS

6 EATING APPLES, CORED, CUT INTO 6 WEDGES EACH

6 PEARS, CORED, CUT INTO 6 WEDGES EACH

1 LOAF FRENCH BREAD, CUBED, WITH CRUSTS

1. To make the cheese, mix the cornstarch and liqueur in a small bowl until all the liqueur has been absorbed.

2. Rub the sides and bottom of the saucepan with the cut side of the garlic. Discard the garlic.

3. Heat the wine in the saucepan until it begins to simmer. Slowly add the grated cheeses. Stirring constantly, add the liqueur mixture until the fondue has thickened, about 4 minutes. Add the mustard, salt, cayenne, and nutmeg.

The cheese may separate if the fondue is boiled or reheated.

12 SERVINGS

SERVICE: Serve in a fondue pot with long fondue forks or skewers for dipping. Place the veggies, fruit, and bread in decorative bowls around the fondue.

COOK'S TIP: For a Southwestern fondue, replace the Gruyère and Emmentaler with Monterey Jack; for an Italian fondue, we like Gorgonzola; for an English fondue, replace the cheeses with Cheddar and substitute ale for the wine.

Swordfish Brochettes with Lime and Ginger

KITCHENWARE: grater, chef's knife, pepper mill, whisk, medium stainless-steel bowl, slotted spoon, 24 heat-resistant skewers, nonstick medium baking pan

PREPARATION TIME: 20 minutes

MARINATING TIME: 2 hours (no longer)

COOKING TIME: 10 minutes

DO-AHEAD: The marinade can be made up to 3 days ahead. Cover tightly and refrigerate. Prepare the cherry tomatoes, zucchini, bell pepper, and parsley the day before. Cover and refrigerate.

MARINADE:

½ CUP LIME JUICE

1 TEASPOON GRATED LIME ZEST

3 TABLESPOONS VIRGIN OLIVE OIL

1 TEASPOON HONEY

½ TEASPOON GROUND CUMIN

1½ TEASPOONS MINCED FRESH GINGER

¼ TEASPOON SALT

⅛ TEASPOON FRESHLY GROUND PEPPER

BROCHETTES:

1½ POUNDS SWORDFISH STEAK,
¾ INCH THICK, CUT INTO 48 PIECES

1 PINT MARBLE-SIZE CHERRY TOMATOES, STEMMED

2 LARGE ZUCCHINI, HALVED LENGTHWISE, CUT INTO 48 CRESCENTS, ½ INCH EACH

FRESHLY GROUND PEPPER TO TASTE

GARNISH:

2 TABLESPOONS DICED RED BELL PEPPER

2 TEASPOONS CHOPPED FRESH FLAT-LEAF PARSLEY

1.   To make the marinade, whisk the ingredients in the stainless-steel bowl.

2.   Place the swordfish pieces in the marinade. Marinate for 2 hours.

Do not overmarinate. The lime juice will break down the fish.

3. Preheat the oven to 350 degrees.

4. Remove the swordfish from the marinade with a slotted spoon. Skewer each brochette as follows: cherry tomato, zucchini, fish, cherry tomato, zucchini, fish.

5. Place the brochettes on the baking pan. Season the brochettes with freshly ground pepper and bake for 10 minutes. Serve warm.

12 SERVINGS

SERVICE: Arrange the brochettes on a platter. Decorate with the red pepper and parsley.

COOK'S TIPS:

❖ Tuna and halibut are good substitutes for swordfish.

❖ Brochettes can also be barbecued.

❖ Serve the brochettes over a bed of couscous as a main course.

Spinach and Pine Nut Pizzetta

PREMADE PIZZA CRUSTS HAVE MADE IT EASY TO PREPARE DELICIOUS PIZZA AT HOME. THE COMBINATION OF RED ONION, PANCETTA, AND PINE NUTS MAKES THIS PIZZETTA IRRESISTIBLE.

KITCHENWARE: pastry brush, baking sheet, chef's knife, grater, large sauté pan

PREPARATION TIME: 20 minutes

COOKING TIME: 10 minutes

BAKING TIME: 15 minutes

DO-AHEAD: Sauté the pancetta, thaw and drain the spinach, slice the onion, grate the cheese, and pit and chop the olives the day before. Remember: cover and refrigerate all Do-Ahead ingredients. Bring to room temperature before using.

FOUR 6-INCH PREMADE PIZZA CRUSTS (BOBOLI)

$^1/_2$ CUP VIRGIN OLIVE OIL

$^1/_4$ POUND PANCETTA (OR BACON), FINELY CHOPPED

ONE 10-OUNCE BOX FROZEN SPINACH, THAWED AND DRAINED WELL

1 RED ONION, THINLY SLICED

7 OUNCES MOZZARELLA CHEESE, GRATED

$^1/_4$ CUP PITTED NIÇOISE OLIVES, CHOPPED

$^1/_2$ CUP PINE NUTS

1. Preheat the oven to 400 degrees.

2. Brush the top and bottom of the pizza crusts with olive oil and place the crusts on the baking sheet.

3. Sauté the pancetta in the large pan to render the fat. Remove the pancetta, leaving the fat in the pan.

4. Add the spinach and onion to the pan and cook for 4 minutes. Pile the pancetta, spinach, onion, cheese, and olives on the pizzas. Sprinkle with the pine nuts.

5. Bake for 12 to 15 minutes, until the bottoms are crisp and the cheese melts.

SERVICE: Cut each pizzetta into 6 wedges. Serve 2 wedges per person.

COOK'S TIPS:

❖ Create Pizzetta Primavera with the Eggplant Caponata (page 32) and grated cheese—mozzarella or Havarti.

❖ Try fresh tomatoes, basil, and mozzarella for other toppings.

❖ Substitute Black Forest or Westphalian ham for the pancetta.

Roasted Pork Tenderloin with Plum Sauce on Cilantro Crisps

WE DEVELOPED THIS RECIPE FOR A LUAU AND, AS OFTEN HAPPENS IN THE KITCHEN AT TAPPAN HILL, ADDED IT TO OUR REGULAR MENU. TOPPING THE PORK WITH THIS HEAVENLY PLUM SAUCE CREATES A DELIGHTFUL CONTRAST BETWEEN THE TARTNESS IN THE SAUCE AND THE SWEETNESS OF THE HONEY MUSTARD.

KITCHENWARE: chef's knife, large mixing bowl, pastry brush, pepper mill, roasting pan, instant meat thermometer

PREPARATION TIME: 10 minutes (not including Plum Sauce)

MARINATING TIME: at least 2 hours

COOKING TIME: 40 to 45 minutes

DO-AHEAD: Prepare the marinade and marinate the pork the day before.

2 TEASPOONS SOY SAUCE

1 TEASPOON DIJON MUSTARD

2 TEASPOONS HONEY

1 CLOVE GARLIC, MINCED

1 1/2 POUNDS PORK TENDERLOIN, IN ONE PIECE

FRESHLY GROUND PEPPER

1 RECIPE PLUM SAUCE (RECIPE FOLLOWS)

GARNISH:

1/4 CUP CHOPPED SCALLIONS

1. Mix the soy sauce, mustard, honey, and garlic in the mixing bowl.

2. Add the pork, brush well with the marinade, and sprinkle with pepper. Marinate for at least 2 hours, covered, in the refrigerator.

3. Preheat the oven to 350 degrees.

4. Fold the tail of the tenderloin under the roast to ensure even cooking and place in the pan. Roast the pork for 40 to 45 minutes, until the inside temperature reaches 160 degrees.

5. While the pork roasts, make the Plum Sauce.

12 SERVINGS

SERVICE: Thinly slice the pork on the bias. Place each piece on a Cilantro Toast Crisp (page 11), top with Plum Sauce, sprinkle with chopped scallions, and serve warm.

COOK'S TIPS:

- ❖ Ask the butcher to remove the silver skin on top of the tenderloin. This membrane does not tenderize in cooking.

- ❖ Barbecue the marinated pork and serve over seasoned rice for a delicious main course.

PLUM SAUCE

KITCHENWARE: chef's knife, small saucepan, vegetable peeler, food processor

PREPARATION TIME: 10 minutes

COOKING TIME: 10 minutes

DO-AHEAD: The Plum Sauce can be made up to 3 weeks in advance. Refrigerate, tightly covered.

$1/4$ CUP CHOPPED ONION	$1/2$ CUP TOMATO SAUCE
$1/4$ CUP CHOPPED, PEELED CARROTS	2 TABLESPOONS TARRAGON VINEGAR
$1/4$ CUP APPLESAUCE	3 DROPS TABASCO SAUCE
$1/2$ CUP BROWN SUGAR	DASH OF CAYENNE
$1/4$ TEASPOON MINCED FRESH GINGER	

1. Put the onion and carrots in the bowl of the food processor. Process until the vegetables are minced.

2. Put the vegetables, applesauce, sugar, ginger, tomato sauce, and vinegar in the saucepan. Simmer for 10 minutes. Add the Tabasco and cayenne and stir well.

COOK'S TIPS:

- ❖ Baking ham, glazed with this sauce, is piquant, golden, and crisp.
- ❖ We love the sauce with roast chicken or duck.

Eggplant Caponata

THE SAVORY SPICES AND VIBRANT COLOR OF EGGPLANT CAPONATA ARE REMINISCENT OF THE CUISINE OF SOUTHERN ITALY.

KITCHENWARE: small mixing bowl, large sauté pan, chef's knife, pepper mill, colander, baking sheet, mixing spoon, paper toweling

PREPARATION TIME: 30 minutes

COOKING TIME: 14 minutes

DO-AHEAD: Eggplant Caponata can be made up to 2 days in advance; however, do not add the capers and the caper juice or the flavors will become too intense. Before serving, add the capers and juice and simmer the caponata for 5 minutes. Reseason to taste.

1 QUART COLD WATER

1 MEDIUM EGGPLANT, DICED

2 TABLESPOONS SALT

2 TABLESPOONS DICED ONION

1/2 CUP DICED RED BELL PEPPER

1/4 CUP DICED CELERY

2 TABLESPOONS VIRGIN OLIVE OIL

2 CLOVES GARLIC, MINCED

1 1/2 CUPS CANNED WHOLE TOMATOES, WITH THEIR JUICE

1 TEASPOON CHOPPED FRESH OREGANO OR BASIL

2 TABLESPOONS CAPERS

1 TABLESPOON CAPER JUICE

1/4 CUP PITTED KALAMATA OLIVES, CHOPPED

1/2 TEASPOON FRESHLY GROUND PEPPER

GARNISH:

2 TEASPOONS CHOPPED FRESH FLAT-LEAF PARSLEY

1. Put the cold water in a mixing bowl and add the eggplant. Add the salt and soak the eggplant for 15 minutes. Drain the eggplant, rinse with cold water to remove the salt, and pat dry with paper toweling.

   Soaking eggplant with salt removes the bitterness from the vegetable.

2. Sauté the onion, bell pepper, eggplant, and celery for 8 minutes in the olive oil. Add the garlic and cook for 1 minute more.

3. Add the tomatoes and their juice, the oregano or basil, capers, caper juice, and olives. Season with pepper. Simmer the caponata for 5 minutes, until all the flavors have blended.

12 SERVINGS

SERVICE: Spoon the Eggplant Caponata into a serving bowl and garnish with the parsley. (Using a white bowl will accent the colors of the vegetables.) Serve with Sesame Pita Crisps (page 34).

COOK'S TIPS:

- ❖ A must for any antipasto!

- ❖ The Eggplant Caponata can be tossed with pasta, used as a filling for vegetable lasagna, or served as a side dish for simple roasts.

- ❖ If refrigerated, reseason the Eggplant Caponata to taste when reheated.

KITCHENWARE: small saucepan, chef's knife, baking sheet, pastry brush

PREPARATION TIME: 10 minutes

BAKING TIME: 10 minutes

DO-AHEAD: Make the Pita Crisps several days in advance and store in the refrigerator or freezer, tightly covered. Recrisp in a 350-degree oven before serving.

SIX 6-INCH PITA BREADS   **2 TABLESPOONS SESAME SEEDS**
1 TABLESPOON SWEET BUTTER, MELTED

1. Preheat the oven to 400 degrees.

2. Cut each pita into 8 pielike wedges. Place on the baking sheet.

3. Brush the top of the wedges with butter and sprinkle with sesame seeds. Bake for 10 minutes, until golden brown.

12 SERVINGS

COOK'S TIPS:

❖ Add minced garlic to the butter before brushing the pita to create a great substitute for garlic bread.

❖ Sesame Pita Crisps are wonderful with Garlic-Scented Gouda Cheese (page 12) and Seviche of Shrimp (page 14).

Chapter 2

Soups and Salads

Soup is the quintessential comfort food. Chilled, it is the perfect summertime thirst quencher. Thick, steamy soup, replete with chunks of vegetables and meats, is the ideal remedy for a long, cold wintry day. Thinking cabbage borscht or minestrone, we raid the market for the necessary ingredients before the roads are closed to all but snowplows.

The heavily perfumed aroma of onion, cabbage, and tomatoes fills every corner of the house as the simmering cabbage borscht's bouquet intensifies. Complete the menu with a salad of Greens, Wild Mushrooms, and Shaved Cheese and warm crackling loaves of Rosemary Bread.

Salads play a major role in our menus. They are no longer thought of as just a side dish with dinner. Dried pears, spicy walnuts, smoky pancetta, and slices of grilled beef are just a few of the foods you can add to transform the greens into an appetizer or a main course.

We use salad greens as a "bed" for many of the foods in our wedding recipes. A bed of wild greens complements our Garlicky Shrimp. Add thinly sliced steamed new potatoes to greens, dress them with balsamic vinaigrette, and scatter chunks of rare tuna over the top. This innovative salad is a favorite in our kitchen. When planning dinner, use your imagination. An intriguing salad may provide the perfect appetizer, side dish, or main course.

Green Minestrone with Spinach and Broccoli Rabe

KITCHENWARE: chef's knife, medium saucepan, mixing spoon, ladle, grater

PREPARATION TIME: 20 minutes

COOKING TIME: 25 to 30 minutes

DO-AHEAD: Make the soup the day before, through step 2. Refrigerate, covered. Before serving, add the broccoli rabe and heat until hot.

3 TABLESPOONS SWEET BUTTER

1 LARGE ONION, DICED

4 LARGE SHALLOTS, DICED

4 CUPS CHICKEN BROTH (FRESH OR CANNED, UNSALTED)

3 LARGE BAKING POTATOES, PEELED AND DICED

1 LARGE TOMATO, SEEDED AND DICED

1/2 TEASPOON DRIED BASIL

1/2 BAY LEAF

1/4 TEASPOON DRIED OREGANO

2 TABLESPOONS TOMATO PASTE

1 BUNCH BROCCOLI RABE, TOP LEAVES AND FLORETS ONLY, CHOPPED

GARNISH:

1/4 CUP GRATED PARMESAN CHEESE

1. Heat the butter in the saucepan. Sauté the onion and shallots until soft and translucent, about 3 minutes.

2. Add the broth, potatoes, tomato, basil, bay leaf, oregano, and tomato paste. Simmer the soup uncovered for 15 to 20 minutes, until the potatoes are not resistant to the tines of a fork.

3. Add the broccoli rabe and cook for 3 minutes more.

4 SERVINGS

SERVICE: Serve the soup hot, garnished with Parmesan cheese.

COOK'S TIPS:

❖ Use this soup as a base for other vegetables (carrots, peas, beans).

❖ Add any bite-size pastas (corkscrew, rotelle, orzo) for a heartier soup.

Black Bean Soup with Kielbasa

When one of our brides at Tappan Hill told us it was an old tradition to serve Black Bean Soup and Kielbasa at family weddings, we developed this robust, mouth-watering version for her. It was so successful, we quickly added it to our list of favorite soups.

KITCHENWARE: colander, large saucepan, chef's knife, grater, small mixing bowl, food processor, ladle

PREPARATION TIME: 1 hour (includes time for beans to soak)

COOKING TIME: 2 hours

DO-AHEAD: Make the soup 2 days ahead, cover, and store in the refrigerator. This soup can also be made in stages, depending on your time constraints. Soak the beans 4 days in advance, make the soup base 3 days in advance, add the kielbasa 2 days before serving. Refrigerate, covered. Warm the soup in the top of a stainless-steel double boiler before serving.

8 OUNCES DRY BLACK BEANS (HALF A 16-OUNCE BAG)

2 TABLESPOONS VIRGIN OLIVE OIL

1 MEDIUM ONION, FINELY CHOPPED

1 MEDIUM RED BELL PEPPER, FINELY CHOPPED

3 CLOVES GARLIC, MINCED

2 TEASPOONS CHILI POWDER

1/2 TEASPOON GROUND CUMIN

1/4 TEASPOON DRIED OREGANO

PINCH OF CAYENNE

1/2 BAY LEAF

1 TABLESPOON BROWN SUGAR

5 CANNED PLUM TOMATOES WITH 2 CUPS OF THE JUICE

9 CUPS WATER

1/2 POUND KIELBASA, CUT INTO CHUNKS

GARNISH:

1 1/2 TABLESPOONS CHOPPED FRESH FLAT-LEAF PARSLEY

1/2 CUP FINELY CHOPPED RED ONION

1/2 CUP GRATED JALAPEÑO MONTEREY JACK CHEESE

1 CUP SOUR CREAM

1. To prepare the beans: Place in the saucepan with water to cover and let stand for 1 hour. (You may also soak the beans in 4 cups of cold water overnight.) Drain and rinse the beans for either method.

2. Heat the olive oil in the saucepan. Sauté the onion and red bell pepper until soft, about 3 minutes. Add the garlic and sauté for 30 seconds. Add the seasonings. Stir and cook for 1 minute on low heat. Add the sugar, plum tomatoes, tomato juice, and water. Add the drained beans and simmer on low heat for 1¾ hours, or until the beans are soft.

3. Ladle the soup into the food processor in small batches and pulse.

   The consistency of the soup should be a chunky puree.

4. Return the soup to the saucepan and add the kielbasa. Heat until the kielbasa is warmed through and the soup is hot.

4 SERVINGS

SERVICE: Ladle the soup into crocks or huge mugs and garnish with the parsley. Serve the onions, Monterey Jack cheese, and sour cream in separate bowls, each with its own spoon.

COOK'S TIPS:

   ❖   Add chunks of hot dogs or leftover meatballs in place of the kielbasa.

   ❖   Reheat all soups in the top of a stainless-steel double boiler. Reseason to taste.

Sweet Potato and Green Apple Soup

SINCE WE'RE ALWAYS LOOKING FOR NEW WAYS TO USE SWEET POTATOES, WE DEVISED THIS RECIPE FOR SWEET POTATO SOUP. TO BE MORE FANCIFUL AND PROVIDE A NICE CONTRAST TO THE SWEETNESS OF THE POTATOES, WE ADDED TART APPLES AND CURRY.

KITCHENWARE: small paring knife, medium saucepan, chef's knife, pepper mill, food processor, slotted spoon, large bowl, ladle

PREPARATION TIME: 35 minutes

COOKING TIME: 30 minutes

DO-AHEAD: Make the soup the day before, but do not add the cream. Refrigerate. Before serving, rewarm the soup in the top of a stainless-steel double boiler and add the cream. If the soup is too thick after rewarming, add a bit of vegetable broth to thin it.

3 SHALLOTS, FINELY CHOPPED

3 TABLESPOONS SWEET BUTTER

1 LARGE CLOVE GARLIC, FINELY MINCED

2 TEASPOONS CURRY POWDER

1 1/2 POUNDS SWEET POTATOES, PEELED, CUT INTO 1-INCH CUBES

4 CUPS VEGETABLE BROTH

2 GREEN APPLES, PEELED, CORED, AND CUT INTO 1-INCH CUBES

1/8 TEASPOON CAYENNE

1/2 CUP HEAVY CREAM

SALT AND FRESHLY GROUND BLACK PEPPER

GARNISH:

1 1/2 TABLESPOONS SOUR CREAM

1 1/2 TABLESPOONS FINELY CHOPPED CHIVES

1. Sauté the shallots in the butter until soft, about 2 minutes. Add the garlic and sauté for 30 seconds. Add the curry and stir well. Add the sweet potatoes and broth and cook for 10 minutes, until the potatoes are soft. Add the apples and cook for 10 minutes more.

2. With a slotted spoon, place apples and sweet potatoes in the food processor in batches. Add half the liquid and process until pureed. Add additional broth as needed, watching for a medium-thick consistency. Process the rest of the soup. Each time, fill the bowl two thirds full.

Don't overload the processor or the liquid will spill over the top of the bowl.

3. Return the soup to the saucepan and simmer for 5 minutes. Add the cayenne and heavy cream and heat for 2 minutes. Stir well and remove from the heat. Season with salt and black pepper to taste.

    Do not boil after the heavy cream is added or the liquids will separate.

4 SERVINGS

SERVICE: Serve the soup hot, garnished with sour cream and chives.

COOK'S TIPS:

❖   Substitute butternut squash for the sweet potatoes.

❖   To serve the soup as a main course, add chunks of smoked or boiled ham or leftover turkey.

Mom's Chicken Soup . . . The Definitive Remedy

MOTHERS OF EVERY ETHNIC BACKGROUND TRULY BELIEVE CHICKEN SOUP IS *THE* MIRACLE DRUG.

WHETHER IT IS CALLED TORTELLINI IN BRODO OR CHICKEN SOUP WITH MATZOH BALLS,

THE BASIC RECIPE IS THE SAME—AND SO IS THE RESULT! SINCE CHICKEN SOUP

FREEZES SO WELL, KEEP SEVERAL CONTAINERS IN THE FREEZER TO COPE

WITH UNEXPECTED HEALTH CRISES.

KITCHENWARE: large saucepan with lid, tongs, large mixing bowl, chef's knife, pepper mill, ladle

PREPARATION TIME: 35 minutes

COOKING TIME: 1 hour 20 minutes

DO-AHEAD: Make the soup up to 2 weeks ahead and store in the freezer. The soup will also keep quite well in the refrigerator for up to 4 days.

1 CUP ROUGHLY CHOPPED CARROTS	ONE 5- TO 6-POUND CHICKEN, CUT INTO EIGHTHS (OR 6 POUNDS CHICKEN BACKS AND NECKS)
1 CUP ROUGHLY CHOPPED CELERY	
1/2 CUP ROUGHLY CHOPPED PARSNIPS	1/2 BUNCH FRESH DILL
1 LARGE ONION, CHOPPED	1 BUNCH FLAT-LEAF PARSLEY, CLEANED AND TRIMMED
2 LEEKS, CLEANED (WHITE PART ONLY), ROUGHLY CHOPPED	SALT AND FRESHLY GROUND PEPPER
1 BAY LEAF	

1. Put the vegetables, bay leaf, and chicken into the saucepan. Add water to cover and bring to a boil.

2. Lower the heat and partially cover. Simmer the soup for 1¼ hours. When the liquid starts to simmer, a light, frothy foam will rise to the top. Skim the foam from the top with the ladle until none remains.

3. Remove the chicken from the soup and separate the meat from the bones. Shred the chicken and return it to the soup. Add the dill, parsley, salt, and pepper and simmer for 5 minutes.

4 SERVINGS

SERVICE: Serve the soup piping hot with the vegetables and shredded chicken.

COOK'S TIPS:

❖   A layer of fat rises to the top of the soup as it cools. There are two simple ways of removing this fat: 1) Place a double layer of paper toweling over the fat, pat gently, and the fat will cling to the paper. 2) Refrigerate the soup and the accumulated fat will solidify and can easily be removed.

❖   Chicken soup bursting with cooked rice or pasta makes a wholesome meal.

Grandma Anna's Cabbage Soup with Short Ribs

ONE OF OUR FAMILY'S EARLIEST AND FONDEST MEMORIES IS OF GRANDMA COOKING IN HER KITCHEN, STIRRING HER MAGIC RECIPE FOR CABBAGE SOUP. THE FAMILY WOULD DEVOUR A FAVORITE SUNDAY SUPPER OF THIS THICK, STEAMING SOUP SERVED WITH SLABS OF BLACK BREAD AND A CRISP SALAD. GRANDMA'S KITCHEN, BATHED IN THE PUNGENT AROMAS OF CABBAGE, BROWN SUGAR, AND LEMON, MADE EVERYONE FEEL WARM AND SAFE.

THE GREATEST CHALLENGE FOR US WAS FINDING OUT JUST HOW MUCH LEMON JUICE AND BROWN SUGAR CREATED THE PERFECT TANGY TASTE. GRANDMA COULDN'T GIVE THE ANSWER, SINCE SHE ALWAYS MEASURED INGREDIENTS IN THE PALM OF HER HAND. LADEN WITH TOMATOES, CABBAGE, AND SHORT RIBS, THIS RECIPE IS A COMPLETE DINNER. NOT ONLY CAN IT BE PREPARED IN ADVANCE, BUT ITS FLAVOR TRULY IMPROVES WITH TIME.

KITCHENWARE: chef's knife, pepper mill, large heavy saucepan, ladle, wooden spoon

PREPARATION TIME: 30 minutes

COOKING TIME: 1½ hours

DO-AHEAD: Cabbage soup improves with age. Don't hesitate to make it in advance. It will keep for up to 4 days in the refrigerator and also freezes quite well. As with all soups, be sure to reseason after reheating.

2 LEEKS (WHITE PART AND 1 INCH OF GREEN STEM)

4 TABLESPOONS VIRGIN OLIVE OIL

1 LARGE ONION, DICED

4 CLOVES GARLIC, MINCED

2 QUARTS BEEF BROTH

2½ POUNDS SHORT RIBS

ONE 28-OUNCE CAN PLUM TOMATOES, DRAINED

2 TABLESPOONS TOMATO PASTE

1 LARGE PARSNIP, PEELED AND DICED

2 CUPS FINELY SHREDDED GREEN CABBAGE (ABOUT 1 SMALL HEAD)

¼ CUP FRESH LEMON JUICE

¼ CUP BROWN SUGAR

SALT AND FRESHLY GROUND PEPPER

GARNISH:

½ CUP SOUR CREAM

1. Slice the leeks lengthwise and cut into half circles. Rinse well. Heat the oil in the saucepan and sauté the leeks, onion, and garlic until just softened, about 3 minutes.

   The leeks' green stems are filled with soil. Separate the greens with your fingers and rinse the stems thoroughly under cold running water.

2. Add the broth, short ribs, tomatoes, and tomato paste. Bring to a boil and reduce the heat to low. Simmer uncovered for about 1 hour, until the short ribs are tender.

3. Remove the meat from the short ribs, cut into bite-size chunks, and return the meat to the soup.

4. Add the parsnip, cabbage, lemon juice, and sugar. Simmer for 15 minutes more, until the vegetables are tender.

5. Taste the soup to adjust the sweet and tangy flavors. Add salt and pepper as needed. We love our soup a little on the tart side.

4 SERVINGS

SERVICE: Spoon the soup, vegetables, and meat into deep soup bowls and garnish with dollops of sour cream. Serve with thick slices of hearty bread.

COOK'S TIP: The sweet and sour flavors develop as the soup simmers. The longer the cooking, the more the flavors intensify as the liquid cooks down. Don't attempt to correct the seasonings until the soup has finished cooking.

Greens, Wild Mushrooms, and Shaved Cheese

HAVING HIS AND HER GRANDMOTHERS TO DINNER AT THE SAME TIME CAN CREATE A REAL
CASE OF THE JITTERS. SERVE THIS "KNOCK-OUT" SALAD FOR A FIRST COURSE. IT WILL
LOOK BEAUTIFUL AND IMPRESS THE HARDEST-TO-PLEASE GRANDMOTHER! ARRANGING
WILD MUSHROOMS OVER THE GREENS WITH SHAVINGS OF PARMIGIANO CHEESE
WILL DISPLAY YOUR NEWLY FOUND CULINARY PROWESS!

KITCHENWARE: aluminum foil, food processor or blender, medium bowl, two baking sheets, vegetable peeler, pepper mill, salad spinner, large wooden salad bowl, colander, paper toweling

PREPARATION TIME: 30 minutes

COOKING TIME: 30 minutes

DO-AHEAD: The vinaigrette for the mushrooms can be prepared up to 5 days in advance and refrigerated, covered. To do this, follow steps 1, 3, 4, and 5.

1 POUND WILD MUSHROOMS (SHIITAKE, OYSTER, CREMINI), WASHED, DICED LARGE

3 CLOVES GARLIC, SLIVERED

1/2 TEASPOON CHOPPED FRESH ROSEMARY

1/2 TEASPOON CHOPPED FRESH THYME

1 CUP VIRGIN OLIVE OIL

SALT AND FRESHLY GROUND PEPPER

3 SHALLOTS, UNPEELED

1 1/2 TEASPOONS DIJON MUSTARD

1 TEASPOON FRESH LEMON JUICE

1/4 CUP TARRAGON VINEGAR

1 SMALL HEAD RED-LEAF LETTUCE

1 SMALL HEAD BOSTON LETTUCE

1 LARGE HEAD RADICCHIO

ONE 2-OUNCE PIECE PARMIGIANO-REGGIANO CHEESE

1. Preheat the oven to 350 degrees.

Wipe the mushrooms with a paper towel if they are clean, with no dirt under the cap. "Dirty" mushrooms should be placed in a colander and rinsed until the water runs clean. Pat the mushrooms with paper toweling.

2. In a medium bowl, toss the mushrooms with the garlic, rosemary, thyme, and 2 tablespoons of the olive oil. Season with salt and pepper. Roast on a baking sheet, uncovered, for 15 minutes. Set aside at room temperature.

3. Place the shallots in the foil, drizzle with 1 tablespoon of the oil, and fold the foil to make a small pouch. The closed pouch seals in the juices. Roast for 30 minutes on the second baking sheet.

4. To make the vinaigrette, remove the shallots from the pouch. Peel the skin and puree the shallots in the food processor with their natural juices, the mustard, lemon juice, vinegar, and salt and pepper.

5. With the motor running, add the remaining olive oil slowly, in a steady stream through the feed tube. Stop and scrape the sides to mix all ingredients well.

    Pouring the olive oil slowly through the feed tube of the food processor produces a thick mixture, the consistency of mayonnaise. If you pour the olive oil through the tube too quickly, the marinade will remain liquid and will not cling to the salad.

6. Scrape the Parmigiano cheese into thin shavings with the peeler and set aside.

7. Separate the heads of red-leaf and Boston lettuce. Cut the radicchio in half and remove the core. Wash the greens, break them into bite-size pieces, and dry them in the salad spinner. Toss the greens in the vinaigrette.

    Always dry greens well, until no water clings to the leaves. Wet greens will dilute the salad dressing. For bright, crisp greens, dress the salad just before serving.

4 SERVINGS

SERVICE: Heap the dressed greens in the center of each salad plate. Place the mushrooms over the greens and drape cheese shavings over the mushrooms.

COOK'S TIPS:

❖ Since wild mushrooms can be a bit pricey, you can substitute the whitest domestic mushrooms in the market. The shallots and mustard in the marinade make all mushrooms taste wonderful.

❖ The salad is best when the mushrooms and vinaigrette are served warm.

Arugula, Endive, and Radish Salad with Balsamic Mustard Vinaigrette

THE FINELY CHOPPED HARD-BOILED EGG IS THE SECRET INGREDIENT IN THIS CRUNCHY SALAD. WHEN BOB AND I WERE FIRST MARRIED, WE WOULD ADD HARD-BOILED EGGS TO JUST ABOUT ANY GREEN SALAD WE CONCOCTED. TODAY, WE LOVE THE SUBTLE FLAVOR THE HARD-BOILED EGG ADDS TO THE SLIGHTLY BITTER ARUGULA AND THE TANGY BALSAMIC VINEGAR.

KITCHENWARE: chef's knife, salad spinner, small saucepan, rubber spatula, food processor

PREPARATION TIME: 25 minutes (not including vinaigrette)

COOKING TIME: 12 minutes

DO-AHEAD: Hard-boil and peel the egg up to 2 days in advance. Cover and refrigerate. Do not chop the egg until ready to use it.

1 EGG	**GARNISH:**
2 BUNCHES ARUGULA	2 TEASPOONS FINELY CHOPPED FRESH CHIVES
1 CUP RADISHES	
2 HEADS ENDIVE	1 RECIPE BALSAMIC MUSTARD VINAIGRETTE (RECIPE FOLLOWS)

1. Place the egg in the saucepan and add cold water to cover. Bring the water to a boil, lower the heat, and simmer for 12 minutes. Run the egg under cold water to cool. Peel and finely chop the egg.

   The secret to peeling a hard-boiled egg is to roll it back and forth on a counter to break up the shell.

2. While the egg is cooking, wash and spin dry the arugula. Trim the ends of the radishes and cut them into ⅛-inch-thick circles. Cut the core ends off of the endive and separate the leaves.

SERVICE: Arrange the endive leaves in a circle, like a starburst, with the points facing the rim of the plate. Place the arugula over the endive and add the radishes over the arugula. Dust the salad well with the chopped egg, garnish with chives, and dress with Balsamic Mustard Vinaigrette.

COOK'S TIPS:

❖ Adding a pinch of salt to the water before boiling the egg makes the peeling easier.

❖ Instead of creating an "arranged" salad plate, simply julienne the endive and toss the salad.

BALSAMIC MUSTARD VINAIGRETTE

KITCHENWARE: rubber spatula, pepper mill, food processor

PREPARATION TIME: 2 minutes

DO-AHEAD: Make the vinaigrette up to 1 week in advance and refrigerate, covered.

1 CLOVE GARLIC, PEELED	1 ½ TEASPOONS SUGAR
1 ½ TEASPOONS DIJON MUSTARD	½ CUP VIRGIN OLIVE OIL
1 ½ TABLESPOONS BALSAMIC VINEGAR	SALT AND FRESHLY GROUND PEPPER
1 TEASPOON RASPBERRY VINEGAR	

1. Put the garlic in the bowl of the food processor and process until it is finely minced.

2. Add the mustard, vinegars, and sugar and process for 30 seconds. *Slowly* pour the oil through the feed tube. The sound of the liquid will change from a waterlike swishing to a heavy, "glub-glub" as the dressing thickens. Season with salt and pepper.

COOK'S TIP: Serve the dressing at room temperature with vegetable or meat salads.

Brown Rice Salad with Oranges and Walnuts

THIS RICE SALAD WITH A SIDE OF YOGURT MAKES A GREAT "LUNCH ON THE RUN." ADDING
LEFTOVER MEAT, SEAFOOD, VEGGIES, OR THE GOODIES YOU BROUGHT HOME FROM YOUR
FAVORITE ASIAN RESTAURANT TURNS IT INTO A TIMESAVING SUPPER.

KITCHENWARE: medium saucepan, small bowl, small whisk, small chef's or paring knife, pepper mill

PREPARATION TIME: 15 minutes

COOKING TIME: 35 minutes

DO-AHEAD: Make the rice up to 2 days ahead through step 2 and refrigerate, covered. Bring the rice to room temperature before completing the recipe. Reseason.

²/₃ CUP RAW BROWN RICE

2 CUPS WATER

¹/₄ TEASPOON SALT

1 TEASPOON VIRGIN OLIVE OIL

2 TABLESPOONS WALNUT OIL

2 TEASPOONS LEMON JUICE

¹/₈ TEASPOON GROUND CUMIN

¹/₈ TEASPOON CURRY POWDER

1 TEASPOON HONEY

SALT AND FRESHLY GROUND PEPPER

2 LARGE EATING ORANGES, SECTIONED

¹/₂ CUP WALNUT PIECES

GARNISH:

1 TABLESPOON CHOPPED FRESH
FLAT-LEAF PARSLEY

1. Put the rice in the saucepan and add the water, salt, and olive oil. Bring to a boil, lower the heat, and simmer, covered, for 35 minutes. Uncover the rice and set aside until it is warm to the touch.

   Raw rice triples in volume when cooked. Warm rice absorbs dressing better than cool rice.

2. In a small bowl, whisk together the walnut oil, lemon juice, cumin, curry, and honey. Toss the dressing with the warm rice. Season with salt and pepper.

3. Fold the orange sections into the rice along with half the walnuts.

4 SERVINGS

SERVICE: Mound the rice in a serving or salad bowl. Top with the remaining walnuts and sprinkle with the parsley.

COOK'S TIPS:

❖   To section an orange, cut off both ends. Pare the skin, turning the orange in a circular motion from top to bottom. Make certain to remove the inside white membrane. It tends to cling to the orange flesh and tastes bitter.

❖   Currants and raisins are good additions to this salad.

New Potato Salad

A GOOD FRIEND LEARNED TO MAKE "THE CONSUMMATE" POTATO SALAD WHILE HONEYMOONING

IN CALIFORNIA. POTATO SALAD BECAME PART OF EVERY SPECIAL DINNER HE AND HIS WIFE

PLANNED DURING THE FIRST FIVE YEARS OF THEIR MARRIAGE. DESIGN YOUR

OWN POTATO SALAD: ADD GRILLED CHICKEN, BEEF, OR SHRIMP.

THE RED ONIONS AND FENNEL ADD FLAVOR AND TEXTURE.

KITCHENWARE: medium saucepan, medium bowl, small whisk, chef's knife, pepper mill, grater

PREPARATION TIME: 25 minutes

COOKING TIME: 25 minutes

DO-AHEAD: Make the potato salad dressing 3 to 4 days in advance and refrigerate, covered. Bring the dressing to room temperature and reseason before using. The potatoes can be cooked the day before; however, the salad is at its best when the potatoes are slightly warm. We prefer to cook them 1 hour before dinner.

1 POUND SMALL NEW POTATOES	1 BULB FENNEL
1 LARGE CLOVE GARLIC, MINCED	1/4 CUP DICED RED ONION
1/4 TEASPOON SUGAR	1/4 CUP CHOPPED FRESH FLAT-LEAF PARSLEY
1 TABLESPOON FRESH LEMON JUICE	
2 TEASPOONS ANCHOVY PASTE	2 TABLESPOONS GRATED PARMESAN CHEESE
1 TEASPOON WHOLE-GRAIN MUSTARD	SALT AND FRESHLY GROUND PEPPER
1/2 CUP VIRGIN OLIVE OIL	

1. Put the potatoes in the saucepan with water to cover. When the water comes to a boil, cook for approximately 25 minutes. The texture of the potatoes should be slightly resistant to the tines of a fork.

2. Drain the potatoes and cool to room temperature without pouring cold water over them. Quarter the potatoes.

This method of slow cooling keeps the skins intact.

3. While the potatoes are cooking, place the garlic, sugar, lemon juice, anchovy paste, and mustard in the medium bowl. Whisk well to blend the ingredients. Slowly whisk in the olive oil. The dressing will thicken.

4. Slice the fennel bulb in half lengthwise. Remove the V-shaped core on the bottom. Cut the fennel into thin slices.

4 SERVINGS

SERVICE: Toss the potatoes in a serving bowl with the red onion and fennel. Add the dressing, parsley, and Parmesan cheese. Combine to coat all the ingredients. Season with salt and pepper.

COOK'S TIP: Add leftover beef or chicken to create a satisfying entrée. We love to throw flank steak on the grill, slice it thin on the bias, and mix it with the salad.

Five-Vegetable Slaw with Gorgonzola

KITCHENWARE: vegetable peeler, hand grater with large slicing ridges, pepper mill, medium bowl, small whisk

PREPARATION TIME: 25 minutes

DO-AHEAD: All the vegetable preparation can be done the day before. For crisp vegetables, complete the recipe a few hours before serving.

1/2 CUP VIRGIN OLIVE OIL

2 TEASPOONS DIJON MUSTARD

1/4 CUP FRESH LEMON JUICE

SALT AND FRESHLY GROUND PEPPER

1 CUP GRATED GREEN CABBAGE

1 CUP GRATED RED CABBAGE

1 SMALL CARROT, PEELED AND GRATED

1 YELLOW BELL PEPPER,
SEEDED, THINLY JULIENNED

1 CUP THINLY SLICED RAW SNOW PEAS

1/4 CUP CRUMBLED GORGONZOLA CHEESE

1.   In the mixing bowl, whisk the olive oil into the Dijon mustard until slightly thickened. Add the lemon juice, salt, and pepper and blend well.

2.   Add the vegetables. Toss well to coat all the vegetables with the dressing.

4 SERVINGS

SERVICE: Put the slaw into a serving bowl and top with the crumbled Gorgonzola cheese. A simple white china dish or a glass serving bowl enhances the vegetables' vivid colors.

COOK'S TIPS:

❖   Add any crunchy vegetables to the slaw. Be sure to keep "color" in mind, since this slaw should be an eye-pleaser.

❖   The slaw is a wonderful side dish with grilled beef, chicken, or fish.

Chapter 3

Vegetables, Potatoes, and Pasta

We grew up on overcooked, unseasoned vegetables; basic mashed potatoes; and pasta coated with butter and cream cheese. Obviously, vegetables and starches were an afterthought in our mothers' menu planning. Today, these foods no longer take a back seat in the culinary arena.

Because of the myriad ways to prepare it and the variety of sauces available, pasta is so flexible it can be served as a first course, a main dish, or "on the side."

Vegetables, too, make a satisfying main course. Green and Yellow Beans, Toasted Pecans, and Brown Butter served with Parmesan Crisp Polenta is a vegetarian's delight. Twice Stuffed Baked Potatoes and loaves of warm Onion Bread make a delicious lunch.

Green and Yellow Beans, Toasted Pecans, and Brown Butter

KITCHENWARE: medium saucepan, colander, small paring knife, slotted spoon

PREPARATION TIME: 15 minutes

COOKING TIME: 10 minutes

1 CUP WATER	1 TABLESPOON SUGAR
1/2 POUND GREEN BEANS, TRIMMED	1/2 CUP TARRAGON VINEGAR
1/2 POUND WAX BEANS, TRIMMED	1/2 TEASPOON HONEY
4 TABLESPOONS (1/2 STICK) SWEET BUTTER	1 TABLESPOON FRESH LEMON JUICE
1 1/2 CUPS PECAN HALVES	1 TEASPOON CHOPPED FRESH TARRAGON

1. Bring the water to a simmer in the saucepan. Simmer the beans until crisp, about 3 minutes. Drain the beans.

2. Melt the butter in the saucepan. Cook the pecans over high heat for 3 minutes to flavor and brown the butter. Remove the nuts with the slotted spoon and reserve. Add the sugar, vinegar, honey, lemon juice, and tarragon to the brown butter. Cook over low heat until the sugar dissolves, about 2 minutes.

3. Add the beans to the butter and toss lightly.

4 SERVINGS

SERVICE: Toss the beans gently with the reserved pecans and serve hot.

COOK'S TIPS:

❖ The beans can be stir-fried instead of simmered. Use peanut oil in place of the butter. As soon as the beans are crisp, toss in all the other ingredients.

❖ Walnuts can be substituted for the pecans.

Broccoli, Feta Cheese, and Rice Strudel

PEEK IN OUR FREEZER AND YOU WILL FIND AT LEAST THREE BOXES OF STRUDEL OR PHYLLO
LEAVES. THESE VERSATILE THIN PASTRY LEAVES FORM A FLAKY WRAPPING THAT CAN
BE FILLED WITH BOTH SAVORY AND SWEET COMBINATIONS OF FOODS FROM LOBSTER,
BEEF, SPINACH, AND FETA CHEESE TO DELICATE CINNAMON-SCENTED,
BUTTERY APPLES. ONCE YOU'RE HOOKED ON THE CRUNCHY TASTE OF BAKED,
FLAKY, GOLDEN PHYLLO, EXPERIMENT WITH A MYRIAD OF FILLINGS.

KITCHENWARE: chef's knife, grater, pepper mill, medium sauté pan, medium saucepan, colander, medium mixing bowl, pastry brush, mixing spoon, kitchen towel, baking sheet (preferably nonstick)

PREPARATION TIME: 40 minutes

COOKING TIME: 10 minutes

BAKING TIME: 35 minutes

DO-AHEAD: Make this strudel whenever you have free time; it freezes beautifully. Be sure to bring it back to room temperature before baking.

4 TABLESPOONS (1/2 STICK) SWEET BUTTER

1 LARGE ONION, FINELY CHOPPED

1 CLOVE GARLIC, MINCED

2 CUPS BROCCOLI FLORETS

1/2 CUP BOILING WATER

1/2 CUP FINELY CHOPPED SCALLIONS (BOTH WHITE AND GREEN PARTS)

1 CUP COOKED RICE

1 CUP CRUMBLED FETA CHEESE

1/4 CUP FRESHLY GRATED PARMESAN CHEESE

2 TEASPOONS FINELY CHOPPED FRESH DILL

1 LARGE EGG, BEATEN, RESERVE 1 TEASPOON

SALT AND FRESHLY GROUND PEPPER

6 LEAVES FRESH OR FROZEN PHYLLO PASTRY (IF FROZEN DEFROST IN REFRIGERATOR BEFORE USING)

1. Preheat the oven to 350 degrees. Butter the baking sheet if it does not have a nonstick surface.

2. Melt 2 tablespoons of the butter in the sauté pan. Sauté the onion until soft, about 3 minutes. Add the garlic and sauté until soft, about 30 seconds more.

   Do not brown the garlic; it will become bitter.

3. While the onions are sautéing, cook the broccoli in the boiling water for 3 minutes. Drain and "shock" the broccoli in cold water. The florets should be crisp.

4. Put the onion, garlic, broccoli, scallions, cooked rice, cheeses, dill, and egg (less the 1 reserved teaspoon) in the mixing bowl. Blend well and season with salt and pepper.

5. Melt the remaining 2 tablespoons of butter. Unroll the phyllo leaves. Dampen a kitchen towel and ring out any excess water. Lay 1 phyllo leaf on a work surface. Immediately cover the remaining leaves with the damp towel to keep them from drying out. Brush the leaf with some of the melted butter. Layer and butter the remaining 5 phyllo leaves.

6. Place the broccoli mixture 3 inches from the edge of the phyllo that is closest to you. Fold the end completely over the filling, tucking in the edges on both sides. Roll the phyllo away from you to form a "jelly-roll"-shape strudel.

7. Place the strudel seam side down on the baking sheet. Brush with the remaining melted butter and the reserved teaspoon of beaten egg. Bake for 35 minutes, until golden brown.

4 SERVINGS

SERVICE: Cool the strudel for 10 minutes before slicing to make it easier to handle. Cut the strudel into 1½-inch slices and serve 2 per person.

COOK'S TIPS:

❖ Don't attempt to cut the slices too thin. The dough is very flaky and tends to crumble.

❖ Thaw and drain frozen chopped spinach and use it as a substitute for the broccoli.

Brown Sugar-Glazed Carrots and Brussels Sprouts

THESE VEGETABLES ARE A MUST FOR THANKSGIVING DINNER. BECAUSE OF THEIR POPULARITY, WE OFTEN SERVE THE CARROTS AND SPROUTS YEAR-ROUND WITH ROAST CHICKEN, DUCK, BAKED HAM, OR ROAST PORK.

KITCHENWARE: medium saucepan with lid, chef's knife, grater, colander

PREPARATION TIME: 12 minutes

COOKING TIME: 10 minutes

DO-AHEAD: These vegetables can be made several hours before serving. Reheat them in a stainless-steel double boiler to maintain the crispness of the vegetables and to keep the glaze from burning.

1 CUP WATER	2 TEASPOONS BROWN SUGAR
1 PINT BRUSSELS SPROUTS, CUT IN HALF	1/4 CUP GOLDEN RAISINS
2 LARGE CARROTS, CUT INTO 1/4-INCH ROUNDS ON THE BIAS	2 TEASPOONS MINCED GINGERROOT
3 TABLESPOONS SWEET BUTTER	GARNISH:
1/4 CUP ORANGE JUICE	1/2 TEASPOON GRATED ORANGE RIND
1 TEASPOON ORANGE LIQUEUR (OPTIONAL)	

1. Bring the water to a boil in the saucepan, add the Brussels sprouts, cover, and cook for 3 minutes. Add the carrots and cook, covered, for 3 minutes more. Drain the vegetables and set aside.

2. To make the glaze, melt the butter and add the orange juice and liqueur. Add the sugar and stir until dissolved. Add the raisins and ginger and simmer for 2 minutes more.

   If you don't have orange liqueur, add the grated zest of a small orange to enhance the orange flavor.

4 SERVINGS

SERVICE: Coat the vegetables with the glaze. Sprinkle with the grated orange rind.

COOK'S TIP: For those who aren't Brussels sprout lovers, green beans or sugar snap peas can be substituted.

Garlicky Mashed Potatoes with Frizzled Onions

OUR FAVORITE CURE FOR EXHAUSTION IS A HEAPING DISH OF CREAMY, GARLICKY MASHED POTATOES TOPPED WITH CRISPY FRIZZLED ONIONS. THE POTATOES HAVE THE SAME SOOTHING EFFECT ON US AS A DISH OF DOUBLE CHOCOLATE ICE CREAM: PURE AMBROSIA.

KITCHENWARE: aluminum foil, large stainless-steel saucepan, vegetable peeler, pepper mill, mixing bowl, colander, potato masher or electric beater

PREPARATION TIME: 15 minutes (not including Frizzled Onions)

COOKING TIME: 30 to 35 minutes

DO-AHEAD: Prepare the potatoes early in the day but do not add the sour cream. When ready to serve, reheat the potatoes in the top of a stainless-steel double boiler. When warm, stir in the sour cream.

4 MEDIUM CLOVES GARLIC, PEELED

1/2 TEASPOON VIRGIN OLIVE OIL

6 QUARTS WATER

8 SMALL RUSSET POTATOES (5 TO 6 OUNCES EACH)

1/2 CUP MILK

6 TABLESPOONS SALTED BUTTER, AT ROOM TEMPERATURE

2 OUNCES CREAM CHEESE, AT ROOM TEMPERATURE

1/4 TEASPOON SALT

FRESHLY GROUND PEPPER

1/2 CUP SOUR CREAM, AT ROOM TEMPERATURE

1 RECIPE FRIZZLED ONIONS (RECIPE FOLLOWS)

1. Preheat the oven to 450 degrees.

2. Place the garlic cloves on a 6 × 6-inch piece of aluminum foil. Drizzle with the olive oil. Close the foil to form a tight package. Roast in the oven for 30 minutes.

3. While the garlic is roasting, bring the water to a boil in the saucepan. Peel the potatoes well, removing all blemishes. Put the potatoes in a mixing bowl with water to cover.

4. When the water has boiled, cook the potatoes until soft, about 25 minutes, and drain well. Do not wash the saucepan. While still warm, mash the potatoes with either a hand masher or an electric beater.

5. Remove the garlic from the foil. Cut off the tip of each clove and squeeze the "garlic paste" into the unwashed, large saucepan.

6. Add the milk, butter, cream cheese, salt, and pepper to the garlic. Heat and stir until the mixture is smooth. Blend in the mashed potatoes. Add the sour cream and blend well.

7. Make the Frizzled Onions.

4 SERVINGS

SERVICE: Serve the potatoes piping hot, topped with the Frizzled Onions.

COOK'S TIP: It's okay to have small lumps in your potatoes; they emphasize "home cooking"!

FRIZZLED ONIONS

KITCHENWARE: whisk, medium mixing bowl, chef's knife, pepper mill, medium saucepan, tongs, paper toweling

PREPARATION TIME: 8 minutes

COOKING TIME: 4 minutes

DO-AHEAD: Make the onions early in the day and store them at room temperature. Do not cover or refrigerate or the onions will become soggy. Reheat in a warm oven to recrisp.

2 TABLESPOONS FLOUR	PINCH OF CAYENNE
SALT AND FRESHLY GROUND BLACK PEPPER	1 MEDIUM Vidalia OR OTHER SWEET WHITE ONION, THINLY SLICED
PINCH OF PAPRIKA	1/2 CUP CANOLA OIL

1. Whisk the flour, salt, pepper, paprika, and cayenne in the mixing bowl.

2. Toss the sliced onion lightly in the flour, shaking off any excess.

3. Heat the oil in the saucepan. Fry the onions until golden, 3 to 4 minutes, tossing them constantly with the tongs. Drain the onions on paper toweling.

4 SERVINGS

Continued

❖   These onions make a great snack.

❖   For a delicious hors d'oeuvre, top small baked new potatoes with the onions and grated Cheddar cheese. Warm them in the oven until the cheese begins to melt.

Twice Stuffed Baked Potatoes

A STEAMY, LAVISHLY BUTTERED BAKED POTATO MAKES A DELICIOUS, SATISFYING LUNCH. WHEN
WE ARE REALLY HUNGRY, WE MASH THE POTATO WITH BUTTER (ONCE STUFFED) THEN ADD
LEFTOVER MEATS, VEGETABLES, OR CHEESES. THE POTATO SHELL IS NOW "TWICE STUFFED."

KITCHENWARE: scrub brush, kitchen fork, $1^{1}/_{2} \times 11 \times 7$-inch roasting pan, chef's knife, grater, pepper mill, medium mixing bowl, hand potato masher

PREPARATION TIME: 25 minutes

COOKING TIME: $1^{1}/_{2}$ hours

DO-AHEAD: Make this recipe through the first baking a few hours before serving, put the potatoes in a roasting pan, and set aside at room temperature. Since the mixture will have cooled, increase the final baking time to be sure the potatoes are piping hot.

4 LARGE BAKING POTATOES (7 TO 8 OUNCES EACH)

4 SCALLIONS (GREEN ONLY), SLICED INTO $^{1}/_{8}$-INCH ROUNDS

2 TABLESPOONS GRATED SHARP CHEDDAR CHEESE

2 TABLESPOONS CRUMBLED BLUE CHEESE

3 TABLESPOONS CHOPPED SMOKED HAM

$^{1}/_{2}$ CUP HEAVY CREAM OR MILK

4 TABLESPOONS ($^{1}/_{2}$ STICK) SWEET BUTTER, SOFTENED

FRESHLY GROUND PEPPER

1. Preheat the oven to 400 degrees.

2. Scrub the potatoes, prick them several times with a fork, and bake for $1^{1}/_{4}$ hours. Cool the potatoes for 10 minutes.

3. Cut off 1 inch from the top of each potato. Scoop the potato flesh into the mixing bowl and save the skins. Add the scallions, cheeses, and ham. Toss well, until blended.

4. Add the cream or milk and butter. Hand mash the mixture and season with pepper. Heap the filling back into the potato skins and stand them on end. Put the potatoes in the roasting pan and bake for 10 to 15 minutes, until piping hot.

4 SERVINGS

SERVICE: Serve one potato per person as a main course.

Brown Rice and Roasted Garlic Custard

FINDING DIFFERENT WAYS TO COOK WITH CUSTARD IS ONE OF OUR FAVORITE PASTIMES. THE
SIMPLE COMBINATION OF EGGS AND MILK, THE BASE FOR ALL CUSTARD, CAN EASILY BE
ELABORATED UPON WITH THE ADDITION OF BOTH SAVORY AND SWEET INGREDIENTS.

KITCHENWARE: nonstick cooking spray, four 6-ounce custard cups, small saucepan with lid, aluminum foil, medium mixing bowl, whisk, chef's knife, grater, pepper mill, ladle, 1½ × 11 × 7-inch baking pan, skewer

PREPARATION TIME: 15 minutes

COOKING TIME FOR RICE: 30 minutes

BAKING TIME FOR CUSTARD AND GARLIC: 30 minutes

DO-AHEAD: Prepare this recipe through step 5 several hours ahead. To complete the recipe, gently stir the mixture in each cup and bake. To guarantee its creamy texture, the custard must be freshly baked before serving.

1⅓ CUPS WATER PLUS 2 CUPS HOT WATER

⅓ CUP RAW BROWN RICE

4 LARGE CLOVES GARLIC, PEELED

½ TEASPOON VIRGIN OLIVE OIL

2 LARGE EGGS, BEATEN

1 CUP MILK

1 TEASPOON DIJON MUSTARD

2 TABLESPOONS GRATED GRUYÈRE CHEESE

PINCH OF CAYENNE

⅛ TEASPOON SALT

⅛ TEASPOON FRESHLY GROUND BLACK PEPPER

1. Preheat the oven to 450 degrees. Spray the custard cups with nonstick spray.

2. Bring the 1⅓ cups of water to a boil in the saucepan. Add the rice, cover, lower the heat, and simmer for 25 to 30 minutes, until the liquid is absorbed. Cool the rice.

3. While the rice is cooking, roast the garlic. Place the cloves in the center of a 6 × 6-inch piece of foil. Drizzle with the olive oil. Form a small package, seal the sides, and bake for 30 minutes. Remove the package from the oven and lower the temperature to 350 degrees.

4. Cut off the tip of each clove and push out the garlic paste from the outside skin; press and mash it with the broad side of the chef's knife. Scrape the garlic into the mixing bowl. Add the eggs, milk, mustard, cheese, cayenne, salt, and pepper. Whisk until blended. Add the cooled rice and stir.

5. Ladle the mixture into the custard cups. Make sure to use all of the liquid and have an equal amount of the custard rice mixture in each cup.

6. Place the filled custard cups in the baking pan. Pour 2 cups of hot tap water to come halfway up the sides of the cups. This is a water bath. Bake the custards for 30 minutes. The custard is done when a metal skewer inserted in the center comes out clean.

The water bath keeps the custard moist and creamy as it bakes in the dry heat of the oven.

4 SERVINGS

SERVICE: Remove the custard from the oven and cool for 5 minutes. Run a kitchen knife between the custard and the cup. Invert each cup onto a separate dinner plate.

COOK'S TIPS:

❖ Small diced, cooked vegetables (zucchini, carrots, tiny peas) can be added to the custard. Serve as a starch with meat, fish, or chicken.

❖ Wild rice or small pastas (tubettini) can be substituted for the brown rice.

Long-Grain Saffron Rice and Mushrooms

RICE, CHICKEN BROTH, MUSHROOMS, AND PARMESAN CHEESE ARE WHAT WE CALL COMFORT

FOODS. TOGETHER THEY MAKE A DISH THAT IS BASIC, YET COLORFUL AND TASTY.

KITCHENWARE: medium saucepan with lid, chef's knife, pepper mill, large sauté pan, grater

PREPARATION TIME: 20 minutes

COOKING TIME: 25 minutes

DO-AHEAD: Prepare the rice and the mushroom sauce early in the day. Do not combine the sauce with the rice until ready to reheat before serving. Reheating in the top of a stainless-steel double boiler will ensure the integrity of the recipe.

2 1/2 CUPS CHICKEN BROTH
(FRESH OR CANNED, UNSALTED)

1/4 TEASPOON SAFFRON THREADS

1 CUP RAW LONG-GRAIN WHITE RICE

2 TABLESPOONS VIRGIN OLIVE OIL

2 MEDIUM CLOVES GARLIC, MINCED

1 POUND MUSHROOMS,
WASHED, DRIED, AND QUARTERED

3/4 CUP HALF-AND-HALF OR HEAVY CREAM

SALT

1/4 TEASPOON FRESHLY GROUND PEPPER

1/4 CUP FRESHLY GRATED PARMESAN
CHEESE

1. Bring 2 cups of the chicken broth to a boil in the saucepan. Add the saffron threads and simmer on low heat, until the broth becomes a golden color, about 5 minutes.

2. Add the rice, stirring well, and bring the broth to a simmer. Cover the saucepan and cook the rice for 12 to 15 minutes. The rice will absorb all the broth.

   Removing the rice from the heat as soon as all the broth is absorbed is key. This ensures that the grains will separate easily when fluffed.

3. While the rice is cooking, heat the oil in the sauté pan. Sauté the garlic for 30 seconds. Add the mushrooms and continue to cook for 2 minutes, stirring constantly. Add the remaining broth, the cream, salt, and pepper. Simmer on low for 5 minutes.

4 SERVINGS

SERVICE: Blend the sauce and Parmesan cheese with the rice. Serve piping hot, as an appetizer or with grilled meats, poultry, or fish. Pass extra Parmesan cheese and a pepper mill.

COOK'S TIP: The addition of cooked chicken, lamb, or shrimp turns this rice into a complete one-dish meal.

White Beans, Spinach, and Tomato

THE AROMATIC COMBINATION OF HERBS, WHITE BEANS, SPINACH, AND TOMATO IS SURPRISINGLY
VERSATILE. WE ENJOY IT AS A HEARTY AND NUTRITIOUS MAIN COURSE OR AS A SIDE DISH.

KITCHENWARE: medium saucepan, colander, chef's knife, pepper mill, large sauté pan

PREPARATION TIME: 20 minutes

SOAKING TIME FOR BEANS: 1 hour

COOKING TIME: 37 minutes

DO-AHEAD: Soak the beans the day before serving. Cook the beans and prepare the vegetables a
few hours ahead. If serving cold, complete the recipe and refrigerate, covered. Bring to room
temperature before serving. To serve hot, complete the recipe through step 3. Combine the beans
and vegetables just before heating.

1 CUP DRIED WHITE BEANS

1 BAY LEAF

SALT AND FRESHLY GROUND PEPPER

1/4 CUP VIRGIN OLIVE OIL

4 CLOVES GARLIC, MINCED

1/2 TEASPOON CHOPPED FRESH ROSEMARY

1 TEASPOON BALSAMIC VINEGAR

1 CUP SEEDED AND CHOPPED TOMATOES
(1 LARGE)

5 OUNCES FRESH SPINACH, WASHED AND
CHOPPED (SPINACH IS USUALLY SOLD IN
10-OUNCE BAGS)

1. Put the beans into the saucepan with water to cover. Bring to a boil and simmer for 2
   minutes. Turn off the heat and allow the beans to soak for 1 hour. Drain the beans.

2. Put the beans back into the saucepan with fresh water to cover plus 2 inches more. Add the
   bay leaf, salt, and pepper and simmer for 35 minutes. Drain the beans.

3. While the beans are cooking, heat the oil in the sauté pan. Add the garlic and rosemary and
   cook for 30 seconds on low heat. Add the vinegar and tomatoes and simmer for 5 minutes.
   Add the spinach and cook until wilted, 1 or 2 minutes.

4. Add the drained beans to the vegetables and mix well to blend all the flavors. Season with additional salt and pepper to taste.

4 SERVINGS

SERVICE: The beans can be served either hot or at room temperature. The recipe can be doubled and served as a vegetarian main dish.

COOK'S TIPS:

- ❖ The white beans will be a little crisp when finished. For a softer bean, increase the cooking time.

- ❖ Tequila Grilled Shrimp (page 223) and these beans make a delicious lunch or supper.

Penne Pasta, Sun-Dried Tomatoes, Arugula, and Black Olives

PIQUANT SUN-DRIED TOMATOES, SPUNKY NIÇOISE OLIVES, AND THE PERFUME OF BASIL AND ARUGULA SUGGEST THE WARM CUISINE OF SOUTHERN ITALY. WE DISCOVERED THIS PASTA DURING AN UNBELIEVABLY DELICIOUS LUNCH IN A TINY, OBSCURE RESTAURANT IN SAN PIETRO. AFTER A LOT OF COAXING, WE TALKED THE CHEF INTO PARTING WITH THE RECIPE.

KITCHENWARE: small saucepan, large saucepan, colander, large mixing bowl, medium sauté pan, chef's knife, pepper mill, food processor, grater

PREPARATION TIME: 25 minutes

COOKING TIME: 20 minutes

DO-AHEAD: Make the sauce early in the day. Reheat it in the top of a stainless-steel double boiler, over simmering water. Just before serving, cook the pasta and toss it with the olive oil. Fit a colander over a saucepan of simmering water to keep the pasta warm.

SAUCE:

2 CUPS WATER

1 ½ CUPS SUN-DRIED TOMATOES (ABOUT 3 OUNCES)

¾ CUP PITTED BLACK OLIVES (NIÇOISE OR GAETA)

1 LARGE BUNCH BASIL, LEAVES ONLY

1 LARGE BUNCH ARUGULA

½ CUP VIRGIN OLIVE OIL

10 OUNCES MUSHROOMS, CUT INTO ¼-INCH SLICES

3 LARGE CLOVES GARLIC, MINCED

½ TEASPOON FRESHLY GROUND PEPPER

PASTA:

6 QUARTS WATER

½ TABLESPOON SALT

1 POUND DRY PENNE PASTA

1 TABLESPOON VIRGIN OLIVE OIL

GARNISH:

¼ CUP FRESHLY GRATED PARMESAN CHEESE

1. To make the sauce, bring the water to a boil in the smaller saucepan. Turn off the heat and soak the sun-dried tomatoes for 5 minutes; drain the tomatoes.

2. Place the sun-dried tomatoes and pitted olives in the bowl of the food processor, process for 20 seconds and reserve.

3. Rinse the basil and arugula leaves, pat dry, and chop into large pieces. Set aside.

4. To make the pasta, bring the water to a boil in the large saucepan. Add the salt and the pasta. Cook for 12 minutes, stirring occasionally. Drain the pasta through the colander and rinse quickly with hot water. Toss the pasta and olive oil in the mixing bowl. Then put it into the large saucepan.

5. While the pasta cooks, complete the sauce. Heat the olive oil in the sauté pan. Add the mushrooms and garlic and sauté for 1 minute. Add the basil and arugula and sauté for 30 seconds more. Add the sun-dried tomatoes, olives, and pepper.

6. Add the sauce to the pasta and toss to mix well. Reheat at low temperature, stirring constantly.

4 SERVINGS

SERVICE: Serve the pasta piping hot, from a large platter or on individual plates, garnished with the grated Parmesan cheese.

COOK'S TIPS:

❖ Add cooked vegetables, shrimp, and/or scallops in step 5 for variety.

❖ The pasta can be served as an appetizer as well as a main course.

Fettucini and Prosciutto

PLEASING OUR CHILDREN IS EASY. ALL WE HAVE TO DO IS COOK THEIR FAVORITE DINNER OF

FETTUCINI NOODLES MIXED WITH HEAVY CREAM, FLECKS OF PROSCIUTTO, AND

PARMESAN CHEESE, AND WE CAN DO NO WRONG.

KITCHENWARE: large saucepan, colander, large mixing bowl, large sauté pan, whisk, chef's knife, small mixing bowl, grater, pepper mill

PREPARATION TIME: 25 minutes

COOKING TIME: 18 minutes

DO-AHEAD: Pasta: you can hold the fettucini, tossed with olive oil, in a colander over a saucepan of simmering water for up to 15 minutes. Sauce: steps 2 and 3 can be done 30 minutes before serving. Steps 4 and 5 should be completed just before the sauce is tossed with the pasta.

PASTA:

6 QUARTS WATER

1/2 TABLESPOON SALT

1 POUND DRY FETTUCINI

1 TABLESPOON VIRGIN OLIVE OIL

SAUCE:

8 TABLESPOONS (1 STICK) SWEET BUTTER

2 SHALLOTS, MINCED

1 1/2 CUPS HEAVY CREAM

1/2 CUP FRESHLY GRATED PARMESAN CHEESE

2 EGG YOLKS

1/4 POUND PROSCIUTTO, THINLY SLICED AND JULIENNED

1/4 TEASPOON FRESHLY GROUND PEPPER

3 TABLESPOONS CHOPPED FRESH FLAT-LEAF PARSLEY

1. To cook the pasta, bring the water to a boil in the large saucepan and add the salt and fettucini. Cook for 13 minutes. Drain and rinse quickly with cold water. Toss the fettucini and the olive oil in the large mixing bowl.

2. To make the sauce, heat the butter in the sauté pan. Add the shallots and sauté for 2 minutes over low heat.

3. Add the cream and ¼ cup of the Parmesan cheese. Heat the sauce on low.

4. Whisk the egg yolks in the small bowl. Whisk ½ cup of the hot cream mixture into the egg yolks. Add this mixture to the sauté pan. Turn off the heat and whisk until the sauce thickens slightly.

Do not boil the sauce or the eggs will scramble.

5. Add the pasta, prosciutto, pepper, and parsley. Warm over low heat, stirring constantly.

4 SERVINGS

SERVICE: Sprinkle the pasta with the remaining Parmesan cheese and serve as an appetizer or a main course.

COOK'S TIPS:

❖ To reduce the fat content in the recipe, substitute milk for the heavy cream.

❖ Add blanched vegetables (asparagus, broccoli, snow peas, or a mixture of peppers) for a pasta primavera.

Parmesan Crisp Polenta

AFTER MUCH EXPERIMENTING IN THE KITCHEN, WE DISCOVERED A GREAT REASON (AND RECIPE)

TO GET OVER OUR CHILDHOOD ANTIPATHY TO CORNMEAL. THIS CRISP,

GOLDEN POLENTA IS HEAVENLY.

KITCHENWARE: grater, medium saucepan, small mixing bowl, whisk, wooden spoon, 8-inch pie plate, 9 × 13-inch baking pan, pastry brush

PREPARATION TIME: 5 minutes

COOKING TIME: 15 minutes

REFRIGERATION TIME: 2 hours

BAKING TIME: 10 minutes

DO-AHEAD: The polenta can be made through step 3 up to a day ahead and kept, covered, in the refrigerator. Bring back to room temperature before completing the recipe.

4 CUPS WATER	1 TABLESPOON SWEET BUTTER, MELTED
1 CUP CORNMEAL	4 TABLESPOONS FRESHLY GRATED
1 TEASPOON SALT	PARMESAN CHEESE

1. Bring 3 cups of the water to a boil in the saucepan. Separately, whisk the cornmeal with the remaining cup of water and stir well. Add the salt to the boiling water. Stir the cornmeal and pour it into the boiling water. Keep stirring until the mixture thickens, about 5 minutes.

2. Lower the heat and continue to cook the polenta for 10 minutes more, stirring often with a wooden spoon. Brush the pie plate with the melted butter.

3. Pour the polenta into the pie plate. Cover and refrigerate for 2 hours or overnight. Bring to room temperature before continuing.

4. Preheat the oven to 400 degrees and preheat the broiler. Cut the polenta into 4 pie-shape wedges. Invert the wedges onto a buttered baking pan.

If your oven and broiler are in the same unit, switch to the broiler unit after baking the polenta.

5. Bake the polenta for 10 minutes. Sprinkle each piece with 1 tablespoon of Parmesan cheese. Broil the polenta for 20 to 30 seconds to brown and crisp the top.

    Keep your eye on the polenta; the cheese burns quickly under the broiler.

4 SERVINGS

SERVICE: This is an ideal starch to serve with roasted or broiled meats.

COOK'S TIP: For a great vegetarian entrée, double the recipe and top the polenta with sautéed mushrooms. Add a crisp salad for a complete dinner.

Chapter 4

Breads

Baking bread is a wonderful activity for a rainy weekend afternoon. The warmth and aromas permeating the kitchen can make you forget the dreariest of days. Best of all, while the dough is rising, there is plenty of time to read the Sunday papers or watch a favorite sporting event.

Since breads freeze so well, you'll have an endless supply to enjoy yourselves or to share with family and friends. Home-baked bread makes a welcome house gift at holiday time or all year round.

Don't be intimidated by the idea of making your own bread. Just follow the steps in each recipe and discover that bread-baking isn't as hard as you thought.

Southwestern Biscuits

KITCHENWARE: fine strainer or sifter, medium mixing bowl, fork, grater, chef's knife, rolling pin, 1½-inch biscuit cutter, baking sheet, cooling rack

PREPARATION TIME: 20 minutes

BAKING TIME: 10 minutes

DO-AHEAD: Make the biscuits early in the day, cool, and store in an airtight container. Biscuits lose their fresh flavor when kept more than a day.

2 CUPS FLOUR	**2 TABLESPOONS FINELY CHOPPED SCALLIONS (GREEN PART ONLY)**
3 TEASPOONS BAKING POWDER	
¾ TEASPOON SALT	**2 TABLESPOONS CHOPPED CANNED ROASTED RED BELL PEPPER**
1 TEASPOON CAYENNE	
⅓ CUP SWEET BUTTER, MELTED	**1 CUP GRATED EXTRA-SHARP CHEDDAR CHEESE**
¾ CUP HALF-AND-HALF	

1. Preheat the oven to 450 degrees.

2. Sift the flour, baking powder, salt, and cayenne into the mixing bowl.

3. Gradually add the remaining ingredients, tossing with a fork until the dough forms a light mound. Turn the dough onto a floured surface and roll the dough to a thickness of ½ inch.

4. Cut the dough into rounds with the biscuit cutter and place them on the ungreased baking sheet. Bake for 10 minutes, until the biscuits are golden brown. Transfer to the cooling rack.

12 TO 14 BISCUITS

SERVICE: Serve 2 biscuits per person.

COOK'S TIP: Add a few drops of Tabasco to the batter for fiery-hot biscuits.

Parmesan-Garlic Breadsticks

START NIBBLING ON THESE CRISP, GARLICKY BREADSTICKS AND YOU WON'T BE ABLE TO
STOP. GREAT WITH LUNCH OR DINNER, THEY ARE ALSO A WELCOME
ADDITION TO ANY COCKTAIL PARTY.

KITCHENWARE: small bowl, instant thermometer, small saucepan, electric mixer with dough hook, rubber spatula, medium mixing bowl, kitchen towel, chef's knife, grater, baking sheet, small sauté pan, pastry brush, cooling rack

PREPARATION TIME: 20 to 30 minutes

COOKING TIME: 2 minutes

RISING TIME: 45 minutes

BAKING TIME: 15 minutes

DO-AHEAD: Make the breadsticks whenever you have time, wrap them well, and store in the freezer. Defrost at room temperature and recrisp in a 350-degree oven for 3 minutes.

OLIVE OIL TO GREASE BOWL AND BAKING SHEET AND TO BRUSH BREADSTICKS	¹/₂ TEASPOON SALT
1 PACKAGE ACTIVE DRY YEAST	²/₃ CUP FRESHLY GRATED PARMESAN CHEESE
¹/₂ CUP WARM WATER (110 DEGREES)	2 CUPS FLOUR
¹/₃ CUP MILK	2 TABLESPOONS VIRGIN OLIVE OIL
1 TEASPOON SWEET BUTTER	3 SMALL CLOVES GARLIC, MINCED
1 TEASPOON SUGAR	

1. Grease the medium bowl and the baking sheet with olive oil.

2. Soften the yeast in the warm water in the small bowl. Scald the milk and butter in the saucepan by bringing the mixture to a boil and immediately removing the pan from the heat. Cool to room temperature.

Water that is too hot will kill the yeast and the sticks will not rise. The water should be slightly warmer than body temperature. Yeast is alive when it begins to ferment and bubble.

3. Place the cooled milk and butter in the bowl of the electric mixer fitted with the dough hook. Add the sugar, salt, $1/3$ cup of the Parmesan cheese, and the yeast and blend lightly.

4. Add the flour, a cup at a time. Knead the dough with the dough hook until the mixture is smooth and elastic, about 5 minutes on low speed. Place the dough in the greased bowl, cover with the towel, and let the dough rise at room temperature until doubled in size, about 20 minutes.

If you do not have a dough hook for your electric mixer, place the flour in a large mixing bowl. With a wooden spoon, make a well in the center of the flour. Place the remaining ingredients in the well and toss until you can form the dough into a ball. Throw the dough onto a floured board and knead until the dough is smooth and elastic, about 7 minutes.

5. Preheat the oven to 400 degrees. Push the dough into a 10×18-inch rectangle with your fingers. Cut the dough in half and then into thirty to thirty-four 5-inch sticks. Place them on the baking sheet, 1 inch apart, and let them rise until doubled again, about 25 minutes. Brush the sticks with olive oil and sprinkle with the remaining Parmesan cheese. Bake for 15 minutes until golden brown.

6. While the breadsticks are baking, heat the 2 tablespoons of olive oil in the sauté pan. Sauté the garlic until soft, about 1 minute. As soon as the breadsticks have baked, brush each hot breadstick with the garlic oil. Cool on the rack.

MAKES 30 TO 34 PIECES

SERVICE: Stand the breadsticks in a napkin-lined woven basket. They are terrific hot or cold.

COOK'S TIPS:

❖   Omit garlic and sprinkle the breadsticks with caraway or sesame seeds.

❖   To vary the recipe, use Cheddar instead of Parmesan cheese.

❖   Keep a supply in the freezer for unexpected guests.

Rosemary Bread

KITCHENWARE: instant thermometer, chef's knife, electric mixer fitted with dough hook, small saucepan, small sauté pan, large mixing bowl, kitchen towel, rubber spatula, 2½-quart casserole, pastry brush, cooling rack

PREPARATION TIME: 20 minutes

COOKING TIME: 3 minutes

RISING TIME: 1½ hours

BAKING TIME: 40 minutes

DO-AHEAD: Make the bread in advance, cool to room temperature, wrap well, and store in the freezer. Defrost the bread at room temperature. Rewarm, lightly covered with aluminum foil, on a baking sheet in a 350-degree oven, about 20 minutes.

1 PACKAGE ACTIVE DRY YEAST

¼ CUP WARM WATER (110 DEGREES)

1 CUP CREAMED COTTAGE CHEESE

3 TABLESPOONS SWEET BUTTER

2 SHALLOTS, CHOPPED

2 TABLESPOONS SUGAR

1 TABLESPOON CHOPPED FRESH ROSEMARY

1 TEASPOON SALT

¼ TEASPOON BAKING SODA

1 EGG, BEATEN

2½ CUPS FLOUR

EGG WASH:

1 EGG BEATEN WITH 1 TABLESPOON HEAVY CREAM

1. Soften the yeast in the warm water for 5 minutes in the bowl of your electric mixer fitted with the dough hook.

   Water that is too hot will kill the yeast and the bread will not rise. The water should be slightly warmer than body temperature. Yeast is alive when it begins to ferment and bubble.

2. In the saucepan, heat the cottage cheese with 1 tablespoon of the butter until lukewarm. Place the chopped shallots with the remaining 2 tablespoons of butter in a small sauté pan and cook until the shallots are soft and transparent, about 2 minutes.

3. Add the shallots, sugar, rosemary, salt, baking soda, egg, 1 cup of the flour, and the cottage cheese to the yeast in the mixing bowl.

4. Knead the dough with the dough hook, on high speed, for 2 minutes. Stop the mixer after 1 minute, and scrape the sides of the bowl with the rubber spatula.

   If you do not have a dough hook for your electric mixer, place the flour in a large mixing bowl. With a wooden spoon, make a well in the center of the flour. Place the remaining ingredients in the well and toss until you can form the dough into a ball. Throw the dough onto a floured board and knead until the dough is smooth and elastic, about 7 minutes.

5. Add the remaining 1½ cups of flour, half a cup at a time, beating well and scraping the bowl after each addition. The dough will be sticky.

6. Place the dough in the large mixing bowl. Cover with a towel, and set the dough aside to rise in a warm place until doubled in bulk, about 1 hour. Punch the dough down a few times.

7. Butter the inside of the casserole. Put the dough in the casserole, cover, and let rise again for 30 minutes. While the dough rises, preheat the oven to 350 degrees.

8. Brush the top of the bread with the egg wash. Bake for about 40 minutes, until golden brown.

4 SERVINGS

SERVICE: Cool the bread for 5 minutes in the casserole. Run a knife between the bread and the casserole. Invert the bread onto a rack. After it has cooled, cut the bread into 1-inch-thick slices.

COOK'S TIPS:

❖ Rosemary Bread is terrific served warm and slathered with butter.

❖ Smoked sliced ham or turkey sandwiched between slices of Rosemary Bread spread with honey mustard is delicious.

❖ Grilled cheese and tomato sandwiches made with Gouda or Muenster cheese become a gourmet delight on this rosemary-flavored bread.

Chocolate-Zucchini Bread

THIS BREAD IS A HEALTH-CONSCIOUS CHOCOHOLIC'S DELIGHT: A BLEND OF COCOA, ZUCCHINI, AND WALNUTS. IT SATISFIES THAT CRAVING FOR CHOCOLATE AND AT THE SAME TIME PROVIDES A TASTY BRUNCH OR TEA DISH.

KITCHENWARE: Bundt pan, nonstick cooking spray, electric mixer, whisk, 2 medium mixing bowls, rubber spatula, grater, fine mesh strainer or sifter, cake tester, cooling rack

PREPARATION TIME: 20 minutes

BAKING TIME: 55 minutes

DO-AHEAD: Make the bread in advance and store, well wrapped, in the freezer. Defrost at room temperature and warm in a 350-degree oven, about 20 minutes.

3 EGGS	1 1/2 TEASPOONS BAKING SODA
1/2 CUP VEGETABLE OIL	1/2 CUP COCOA POWDER
1/2 CUP MILK	2 TEASPOONS GROUND CINNAMON
2 TEASPOONS PURE VANILLA EXTRACT	1 TEASPOON GROUND CLOVES
1 1/2 CUPS SUGAR	1 TEASPOON SALT
2 TEASPOONS GRATED ORANGE ZEST	2 CUPS GRATED ZUCCHINI, SQUEEZED DRY
2 1/2 CUPS FLOUR	1 1/2 CUPS CHOPPED WALNUTS
2 1/2 TEASPOONS BAKING POWDER	

1. Preheat the oven to 350 degrees. Spray the Bundt pan with nonstick cooking spray.

2. In one bowl, beat the eggs, oil, milk, vanilla, sugar, and zest on low speed, until blended.

3. Sift the flour, baking powder, baking soda, cocoa, cinnamon, cloves, and salt together in the second bowl. Make a well in the center of the dry ingredients and place the egg mixture into the well. Blend in the electric mixer until all the ingredients are just incorporated. Stir in the zucchini and nuts.

4. Pour the batter into the Bundt pan and bake for 55 minutes, until the cake tester inserted into the middle of the cake comes out clean. Let the cake rest on the rack for 5 minutes. Invert the Bundt pan, remove the bread, and cool.

10 TO 12 SERVINGS

SERVICE: Serve the bread with softened cream cheese and fruit preserves.

COOK'S TIP: Substitute grated carrot for the zucchini to make a delicious chocolate-carrot bread.

Onion Bread

KITCHENWARE: electric mixer fitted with dough hook, instant thermometer, large mixing bowl, kitchen towel, chef's knife, two 9-inch round cake pans, cooling rack

PREPARATION TIME: 20 minutes

RISING TIME: 1¾ hours

BAKING TIME: 20 minutes

DO-AHEAD: Bake a few of these breads in advance, cool, wrap well, and store in the freezer. Defrost the breads at room temperature and warm in a 350-degree oven, about 10 minutes.

1 PACKAGE ACTIVE DRY YEAST	2½ CUPS FLOUR
1 CUP WARM WATER (110 DEGREES)	2 TABLESPOONS SWEET BUTTER, MELTED
2 TEASPOONS SUGAR	½ CUP COARSELY CHOPPED ONION
2 TEASPOONS SALT	2 TEASPOONS PAPRIKA

1. Butter the mixing bowl. Grease the cake pans.

2. Sprinkle the yeast over the warm water in the bowl of the mixer. Stir until dissolved. Add the sugar, 1 teaspoon of the salt, and 2 cups of the flour. Beat well with the dough hook, until all the ingredients are blended.

   Water that is too hot will kill the yeast and the bread will not rise. The water should be slightly warmer than body temperature. Yeast is alive when it begins to ferment and bubble.

   If you do not have a dough hook for your electric mixer, place the flour in a large mixing bowl. With a wooden spoon, make a well in the center of the flour. Place the remaining ingredients in the well and toss until you can form the dough into a ball. Throw the dough onto a floured board and knead until the dough is smooth and elastic, about 7 minutes.

3. Stir in the remaining ½ cup of flour. Beat on low speed for 7 minutes.

4. Put the dough in the buttered mixing bowl. Cover with a kitchen towel and let the dough rise in a warm place until doubled in bulk, about 1 hour.

5. Punch the dough down and divide it in half. Place the halves in the buttered cake pans. Brush the tops of the breads with the melted butter and sprinkle with the chopped onion.

6. Allow the dough to rise until doubled again, about 45 minutes. Meanwhile, preheat the oven to 450 degrees.

7. Sprinkle the tops of the loaves with the remaining teaspoon of salt and the paprika. Bake for 20 minutes, until golden.

The Onion Breads are small and bake quickly.

4 SERVINGS

SERVICE: Unmold the breads and cool on the rack. Cut into wedges and serve warm.

COOK'S TIP: For a no-fuss snack, try this overstuffed sandwich: Slice each loaf in half. Pile sliced ham, salami, provolone, roasted red peppers, sliced red onion, and roasted garlic over the bottom half. Sprinkle with Balsamic Mustard Vinaigrette (page 51) and cover. Go heavy on the napkins!

Garlic and Onion Focaccia

VERSATILE FOCACCIA—THE BRIDE AND GROOM'S ANSWER TO "WHAT SHALL I SERVE?" AND "WHAT SHALL I BRING?" FOCACCIA—USE IT AS AN HORS D'OEUVRE, TAKE IT ON A PICNIC, SNACK ON IT WHILE WATCHING TELEVISION, OR BRING IT TO A HOUSE-WARMING OR OFFICE PARTY.

KITCHENWARE: 2-cup measuring cup, instant thermometer, electric mixer with dough hook, chef's knife, pepper mill, rubber spatula, medium bowl, kitchen towel, pastry brush, baking sheet, small sauté pan, cooling rack

PREPARATION TIME: 25 minutes

RISING TIME: 1 hour

COOKING TIME: 9 minutes

BAKING TIME: 25 minutes

DO-AHEAD: Make the focaccia ahead and freeze, well covered. Defrost at room temperature and warm in a 350-degree oven, about 6 minutes.

1 CUP WARM WATER (110 DEGREES)	1 MEDIUM ONION, HALF FINELY CHOPPED, HALF CUT INTO 1/8-INCH SLICES
1 PACKAGE ACTIVE DRY YEAST	2 CLOVES GARLIC, FINELY MINCED
1 TABLESPOON SUGAR	1 TEASPOON FRESHLY GROUND PEPPER
3 CUPS FLOUR	1 TABLESPOON CHOPPED FRESH BASIL
2 TEASPOONS SALT	1 TABLESPOON CHOPPED FRESH FLAT-LEAF PARSLEY
6 TABLESPOONS VIRGIN OLIVE OIL	

1. Fill the 2-cup measuring cup with the warm water. Sprinkle the yeast and sugar over the water, blend lightly, and let the yeast stand for 10 minutes, until foamy.

   Water that is too hot will kill the yeast and the bread will not rise. The water should be slightly warmer than body temperature. Yeast is alive when it begins to ferment and bubble.

2. Mix 2½ cups of the flour and the salt in the bowl of the electric mixer. Make a well in the center of the flour and add 3 tablespoons of the oil and the yeast.

3. Knead the batter with the dough hook for 10 minutes. Scrape down the sides of the bowl a few times. Add the remaining ½ cup of flour if the dough is still sticky. (You can expect that it will be sticky.) Turn the dough into an oiled bowl and cover with the towel.

    If you do not have a dough hook for your electric mixer, place the flour in a large mixing bowl. With a wooden spoon, make a well in the center of the flour. Place the remaining ingredients in the well and toss until you can form the dough into a ball. Throw the dough onto a floured board and knead until the dough is smooth and elastic, about 7 minutes.

4. Let the dough rise for 30 minutes in a warm place. Punch down the dough and let it rise, covered, 30 minutes more. Preheat the oven to 450 degrees and brush the baking sheet with oil.

5. While the dough is rising, sauté the chopped onion in 1½ tablespoons of the olive oil for 2 minutes. Add the garlic, sauté for 1 minute, and cool. Sauté the sliced onion in the remaining 1½ tablespoons of oil until translucent, about 5 minutes.

6. Knead the chopped onion and garlic mixture, the pepper, basil, and parsley into the dough until well distributed. Flour your hands and press the dough onto the oiled baking sheet so that the dough completely covers the sheet. Arrange the onion slices over the top. Bake for 20 to 25 minutes, until golden and crisp. Transfer to the cooling rack.

8 SERVINGS

SERVICE: Cut the focaccia across the width into 1-inch strips.

COOK'S TIPS:

❖   For a savory hors d'oeuvre, omit the garlic and onions and slice the focaccia lengthwise. Cover one side with diced prosciutto and pitted niçoise olives. Place the other half over the filling. Cut the bread into 1½ × 1½-inch mini-sandwiches. Arrange on a platter or a flat bread basket.

❖   Warm some olive oil with basil or rosemary. Dip the focaccia into the herbed oil.

Smoked Ham and Swiss Muffins

KITCHENWARE: chef's knife, grater, whisk, 2 medium mixing bowls, rubber spatula, nonstick cooking spray, 12-cup muffin pan, cooling rack

PREPARATION TIME: 20 minutes

BAKING TIME: 20 to 25 minutes

DO-AHEAD: Bake these muffins well in advance and store, well covered, in the freezer; or bake them 2 days ahead and store in the refrigerator. Uncover and bring to room temperature before warming in a 350-degree oven for 6 minutes.

1/2 CUP DRAINED, CANNED, CRUSHED PINEAPPLE	2 1/2 CUPS FLOUR
1 CUP PINEAPPLE JUICE	1 1/2 TEASPOONS BAKING POWDER
2 EGGS, BEATEN	1/2 TEASPOON BAKING SODA
4 OUNCES SMOKED HAM, CUT INTO 1/4-INCH PIECES	1 TEASPOON SALT
	3/4 TEASPOON WHITE PEPPER
2 TABLESPOONS WHOLE-GRAIN MUSTARD	1/2 CUP COARSELY GRATED SWISS CHEESE

1. Preheat the oven to 425 degrees. Spray the muffin pan with nonstick cooking spray.

2. Blend the pineapple, pineapple juice, eggs, ham, and mustard in one mixing bowl.

3. Mix the flour, baking powder, baking soda, salt, pepper, and cheese in the other bowl. Blend the moist ham mixture into the dry flour mixture until it is just incorporated.

4. Spoon the batter into the muffin cups, filling them two thirds of the way to the top. Bake for 20 to 25 minutes, until the muffins are a light golden brown. Transfer to the cooling rack.

12 MUFFINS

SERVICE: Serve these muffins for brunch with fluffy scrambled eggs.

- ❖   The ham and cheese muffins, halved and filled with ham and cheese, are great additions to a picnic or tailgate party.

- ❖   Be creative with the recipe by substituting other smoked meats (turkey or crisp bacon). Monterey Jack or sharp Cheddar cheese work well with turkey and pork.

Apricot-Pecan Biscuits

KITCHENWARE: chef's knife, 12-cup muffin pan, nonstick cooking spray, small bowl, 2 medium bowls, whisk, rubber spatula, cooling rack

PREPARATION TIME: 20 minutes

BAKING TIME: 25 minutes

DO-AHEAD: These biscuits are best baked just before eating. If pressed for time, bake them 1 hour before serving and hold at room temperature.

¹/₂ CUP CHOPPED DRIED APRICOTS	1 TEASPOON ALMOND EXTRACT
¹/₂ CUP RAISINS	2 CUPS FLOUR
¹/₄ CUP BRANDY	2 TEASPOONS BAKING POWDER
2 EGGS	¹/₂ CUP SUGAR
1 CUP MILK	¹/₂ TEASPOON GROUND CINNAMON
¹/₂ CUP ORANGE JUICE	¹/₂ CUP CHOPPED PECAN PIECES
¹/₄ CUP (¹/₂ STICK) SWEET BUTTER, MELTED	

1. Preheat the oven to 350 degrees. Spray the muffin pan with nonstick cooking spray.

2. In the small bowl, soak the apricots and raisins in the brandy (orange juice can be substituted for the brandy) for 10 minutes.

    This is called "plumping" the fruit.

3. Mix the eggs, milk, orange juice, butter, and almond extract in one of the mixing bowls.

4. Mix the flour, baking powder, sugar, and cinnamon in the other bowl. Make a well in the center of the dry ingredients, add the egg mixture, and whisk until just blended. Drain the fruit, stir into the batter, and add the pecans.

5. Fill the muffin cups two-thirds full and bake the biscuits for 25 minutes, until golden. Cool for 5 minutes in the pan, then flip out onto the rack.

12 SERVINGS

SERVICE: Line a basket or bread tray with a colorful napkin. Serve the muffins warm, with fruit preserves.

COOK'S TIP: Substitute any dry pitted fruit for the apricots.

Chapter 5

Fish and Shellfish

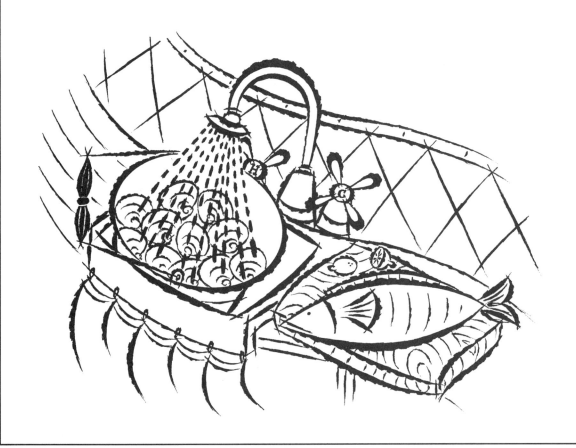

FISH IS "IN." AS WE HAVE BECOME MORE AND MORE HEALTH-CONSCIOUS,
REDUCING OUR FAT AND CALORIE INTAKE, FISH AND SHELLFISH
HAVE BECOME GLAMOROUS FOODS.

IN THE PAST, WE SIMPLY BROILED FILLET OF SOLE, MACKEREL, OR BLUEFISH. MARKETS
NOW OFFER A GREATER VARIETY OF FRESH FISH (TUNA, SWORDFISH, RED SNAPPER)
SPECIALLY PREPARED TO ACCOMMODATE CREATIVE COOKING METHODS
SUCH AS INFUSING THE FISH WITH HERBED CITRUS BUTTERS
OR INTRIGUING VINEGARS.

COMPLEMENT SEAFOOD DINNERS WITH GARLICKY MASHED POTATOES, PARMESAN CRISP
POLENTA, WHITE BEANS, OR PASTA. SERVE A FRESH FRUIT DESSERT
TO COMPLETE A LIGHT, HEALTHY MEAL.

Sautéed Red Snapper with Raspberry Vinegar

EATING COUNTLESS SUCCULENT, HEAVILY PERFUMED RASPBERRIES DURING THE LAZY DAYS OF SUMMER IS A JOY. SAMPLING THE FIRST MORSELS OF THIS RED SNAPPER, ENRICHED WITH RASPBERRY VINEGAR, IS REMINISCENT OF THAT DELICIOUS PASTIME.

KITCHENWARE: chef's knife, pepper mill, large sauté pan, spatula

PREPARATION TIME: 12 minutes

COOKING TIME: 12 minutes

FOUR 6-OUNCE RED SNAPPER FILLETS, ½ TO ⅔ INCH THICK

½ CUP FLOUR, SEASONED WITH SALT AND FRESHLY GROUND PEPPER FOR DUSTING

3 TABLESPOONS VIRGIN OLIVE OIL

3 TABLESPOONS SWEET BUTTER

1 SMALL SHALLOT, FINELY MINCED

¼ CUP RASPBERRY VINEGAR

½ CUP FISH BROTH OR CLAM JUICE

GARNISH:

4 LEMON WEDGES

1 BUNCH WATERCRESS

1. Pat the fish dry and dust it with the seasoned flour.

2. Heat the oil in the sauté pan over moderately high heat. Sauté the fish for 5 minutes on one side. Turn with the spatula, lower the heat, and sauté for about 1 to 2 minutes, depending on the thickness of the fish.

3. Remove the fish to a warmed serving platter. Melt the butter in the pan and sauté the shallot for 3 minutes, until soft. Add the raspberry vinegar and broth or juice. Simmer for 2 minutes and pour over the snapper.

4 SERVINGS

SERVICE: Garnish the red snapper with watercress and lemon wedges.

COOK'S TIP: If raspberries are in season, use them as a garnish, too.

Sautéed Scallops with Bok Choy and Snow Peas

SAUTÉING IN A WOK HAS MANY ADVANTAGES. IT'S QUICK, HEALTHY, AND REQUIRES MINIMAL CLEAN UP.

KITCHENWARE: small mixing bowl, whisk, grater, chef's knife, pepper mill, wok and shovel

PREPARATION TIME: 35 minutes

MARINATING TIME: 2 hours

COOKING TIME: 8 minutes

DO-AHEAD: Make the marinade up to 1 week in advance and refrigerate, covered. Bring the marinade to room temperature before adding the scallops. Chop the vegetables the day before, seal with plastic wrap, and refrigerate.

2 TABLESPOONS HOISIN SAUCE

1 TEASPOON GRATED FRESH GINGER

2 LARGE CLOVES GARLIC, MINCED

3 TABLESPOONS SESAME OIL

1 TABLESPOON ORANGE JUICE

SALT AND FRESHLY GROUND PEPPER

1 1/2 POUNDS SEA SCALLOPS

1 SMALL RED BELL PEPPER, SEEDED AND JULIENNED

2 CUPS SNOW PEAS, JULIENNED

3 CUPS JULIENNED BOK CHOY CABBAGE

GARNISH:

1/2 CUP SLICED SCALLIONS (WHITE AND GREEN PARTS), CUT ON THE BIAS

1. Whisk the hoisin sauce, ginger, half the garlic, half the sesame oil, and the juice in a small bowl. (This is the scallop marinade.)

2. Remove the small muscle-type nob from each scallop. Cut the larger scallops into bite-size pieces. Marinate the scallops for approximately 2 hours in the refrigerator.

   Don't marinate the scallops more than 2 hours; the acid in the marinade will cause the flesh of the fish to break down.

3. Heat the remaining sesame oil in the wok. Stir-fry the red bell pepper for 1 minute. Add the remaining garlic and stir-fry for 20 seconds, tossing frequently. Drain and add the scallops and stir-fry for about 4 minutes over high heat.

    Do not overcook the scallops or they will toughen. The centers should be opaque.

4. Add the snow peas and cabbage and cook for 1 minute, stirring gently.

4 SERVINGS

SERVICE: Remove from the heat and garnish with the scallions. Serve the scallops directly from the wok.

COOK'S TIPS:

❖   Fresh lobster meat or uncooked shrimp, peeled and deveined, are fine alternatives to the scallops.

❖   If bok choy isn't readily available, use Napa cabbage.

Mediterranean Fish Stew

DON'T LET THE LONG INGREDIENTS LIST SCARE YOU AWAY! MEDITERRANEAN FISH STEW IS QUICK AND EASY TO PREPARE. THE RESULT—A DELICIOUS ONE-DISH MEAL LOADED WITH FRESH FISH AND VEGETABLES.

KITCHENWARE: large sauté pan,, chef's knife, pepper mill, vegetable peeler, hard bristle scrub brush, ladle

PREPARATION TIME: 25 minutes

COOKING TIME: 25 minutes

DO-AHEAD: Chop all those vegetables the day before. Refrigerate in airtight containers or well sealed in plastic wrap. (Store each vegetable separately.) The broth can be made a day ahead and refrigerated. Bring the broth to a simmer and add the seafood just before serving.

2 TABLESPOONS VIRGIN OLIVE OIL	1/4 TEASPOON SAFFRON THREADS
2 STALKS CELERY, FINELY CHOPPED	1 BAY LEAF
1 MEDIUM ONION, FINELY CHOPPED	12 CHERRYSTONE CLAMS, SCRUBBED CLEAN
1 MEDIUM CARROT, FINELY CHOPPED	8 LARGE RAW SHRIMP, PEELED AND DEVEINED
2 MEDIUM LEEKS (WHITE PART ONLY), CLEANED AND SLICED	1/2 POUND RED SNAPPER FILLET, CUT INTO BITE-SIZE CHUNKS
1/2 CUP JULIENNED FENNEL	1/2 POUND HALIBUT FILLET, CUT INTO BITE-SIZE CHUNKS
3 CLOVES GARLIC, FINELY MINCED	
1 POUND FRESH TOMATOES, PEELED, SEEDED, AND DICED	SALT AND FRESHLY GROUND PEPPER
2 CUPS FISH OR VEGETABLE BROTH	
1 CUP DRY WHITE WINE	

1. Heat the oil in the sauté pan. Sauté the celery, onion, carrot, leeks, and fennel for about 8 minutes. Add the garlic and sauté for 2 minutes more. Add the tomatoes, broth, wine, saffron, and bay leaf. Cook for 5 minutes.

2. Add the clams and shrimp and cook until the clams begin to open, about 4 minutes. Add the snapper and halibut, and cook for 5 minutes more, until the clams are completely open, the centers of the shrimp are opaque, and the top of the fish flakes when pierced with the tines of a fork. Season with salt and pepper and serve immediately.

Always discard unopened clams before serving.

4 SERVINGS

SERVICE: Ladle the broth into deep soup bowls and add the seafood.

COOK'S TIP: Don't even think of precooking the fish. It has to be done at the last moment and is well worth the effort.

Roasted Herbed Halibut with Tomato and Caper Relish

~

KITCHENWARE: chef's knife, pepper mill, small bowl, baking sheet, pastry brush

PREPARATION TIME: 10 minutes (not including Tomato and Caper Relish)

MARINATING TIME: 25 minutes

COOKING TIME: 10 minutes

DO-AHEAD: If you are really pressed for time, chop the shallots and cilantro ahead. Make sure to store them separately, tightly wrapped, in the refrigerator.

FOUR 6-OUNCE BONED AND SKINNED HALIBUT STEAKS, ABOUT 1 INCH THICK

KOSHER SALT AND FRESHLY GROUND PEPPER

4 TABLESPOONS VIRGIN OLIVE OIL

2 TEASPOONS FINELY CHOPPED SHALLOTS

2 TABLESPOONS FINELY CHOPPED FRESH CILANTRO

2 TEASPOONS FRESH LIME JUICE

1 RECIPE TOMATO AND CAPER RELISH (RECIPE FOLLOWS)

1. Preheat the oven to 400 degrees.

2. Lightly salt and pepper the fish.

3. In the small bowl, mix the olive oil, shallots, cilantro, and juice. Spread over the fish using all the marinade. Cover and marinate for 25 minutes in the refrigerator.

4. Make the Tomato and Caper Relish.

5. Bake the fish for 10 minutes, until the top of the fish flakes when pierced with the tines of a fork.

4 SERVINGS

SERVICE: Remove the fish to a warm platter or individual dinner plates. Serve with the Tomato and Caper Relish.

❖ The halibut can be grilled over very low gray coals.

❖ If there isn't enough time to prepare the Tomato and Caper Relish, serve the fish with fresh lime or lemon wedges.

TOMATO AND CAPER RELISH

KITCHENWARE: chef's knife, pepper mill, small bowl

PREPARATION TIME: 10 minutes

DO-AHEAD: The relish can be made up to 2 days in advance and kept, covered, in the refrigerator. Drain off any watery liquids that form during storage. Reseason the relish as needed.

2 TEASPOONS FINELY CHOPPED SHALLOTS

2 TABLESPOONS VIRGIN OLIVE OIL

2 MEDIUM TOMATOES, CHOPPED; OR 4 CANNED PLUM TOMATOES, DRAINED AND CHOPPED

1/2 CUP FINELY DICED FENNEL

1 TABLESPOON BALSAMIC VINEGAR

1/4 TEASPOON FRESHLY GROUND PEPPER

1 TEASPOON CHOPPED FRESH CILANTRO

2 TEASPOONS DRAINED AND FINELY CHOPPED CAPERS

Put all the ingredients in the small bowl and mix well.

The relish tastes best when the flavors of all the ingredients have time to blend (about 20 minutes).

4 SERVINGS

Roasted Salmon in Horseradish Crust

THE MAGICAL INGREDIENTS THAT HEIGHTEN THE TASTE OF FRESH SALMON ARE WHITE
HORSERADISH, MUSTARD, AND LEMON. COMBINING ALL THREE IN A CRUST FOR
THE SALMON HAS THE ADDED VALUE OF KEEPING THE SALMON MOIST.

KITCHENWARE: food processor, baking sheet, chef's knife, grater, spatula

PREPARATION TIME: 15 minutes

COOKING TIME: 10 minutes to the inch (15 minutes)

DO-AHEAD: Make the horseradish crust in the morning and refrigerate, covered. Bring to room
temperature before spreading over the salmon.

6 TABLESPOONS SWEET BUTTER, AT ROOM
TEMPERATURE

1/2 CUP GRATED WHITE HORSERADISH,
SQUEEZED DRY

2 WHOLE SCALLIONS, FINELY DICED

1/4 TEASPOON WASABI POWDER (CAN BE
PURCHASED IN GOURMET MARKETS OR
ORIENTAL FOOD STORES)

1/4 TEASPOON GROUND GINGER

1/4 TEASPOON DIJON MUSTARD

1/2 CUP DRY UNSEASONED BREAD CRUMBS

1 TEASPOON FINELY CHOPPED SHALLOTS

1/4 CUP FRESH LEMON JUICE

1/4 TEASPOON GRATED LEMON ZEST

PINCH OF CAYENNE

FOUR 6-OUNCE CENTER-CUT SALMON
FILLETS, 1 1/2 INCHES THICK

1/2 CUP WHITE WINE OR VERMOUTH

GARNISH:

4 LIME WEDGES

1. Preheat the oven to 400 degrees.

2. Put the butter, horseradish, scallions, wasabi powder, ginger, mustard, bread crumbs, shallots,
    juice, zest, and cayenne in the bowl of the food processor. Pulse until the ingredients form a
    ball. This is the horseradish crust.

3. Place the fish on the baking sheet and cover with the wine. Spread the horseradish mixture
    over the fillets, about 1/4 inch thick.

4. Roast the salmon for about 15 minutes, or until the top of the fish flakes when pierced with the tines of a fork.

We enjoy our salmon served a little pink.

4 SERVINGS

SERVICE: Garnish the salmon with lime wedges and serve hot.

COOK'S TIP: The salmon is magnificent served on a bed of Garlicky Mashed Potatoes (page 66) or Sautéed Spinach and Leeks (page 281).

Garlicky Shrimp

THERE IS NOTHING AS ENTICING AS THE FRAGRANT AROMA OF

GARLIC SIMMERING IN OLIVE OIL.

KITCHENWARE: chef's knife, large sauté pan, medium mixing bowl

PREPARATION TIME: 20 minutes

COOKING TIME: 10 minutes

2 TABLESPOONS VIRGIN OLIVE OIL

1 1/2 POUNDS RAW LARGE SHRIMP, PEELED AND DEVEINED (ABOUT 32 SHRIMP)

3 LARGE CLOVES GARLIC, MINCED

1/4 CUP DRY VERMOUTH OR DRY WHITE WINE

3 CUPS IMPORTED CANNED PLUM TOMATOES WITH THEIR JUICE, CHOPPED

2 TABLESPOONS CHOPPED FRESH FLAT-LEAF PARSLEY

1. Heat the olive oil in the sauté pan. Add the shrimp and cook, tossing, until the shrimp turn bright pink, about 3 minutes. Thirty seconds before the shrimp are finished, add the garlic. Put the Garlicky Shrimp into the mixing bowl.

   Cook shrimp in two batches if all shrimp don't fit into the sauté pan without touching.

2. Add the vermouth to the sauté pan and simmer for 30 seconds. Add the tomatoes and parsley and simmer for 5 minutes.

3. Return the shrimp to the sauté pan and toss well in the sauce. Warm the Garlicky Shrimp on low heat for 1 minute.

   Do not overcook the shrimp; they will toughen.

4 SERVINGS

SERVICE: Serve the shrimp over Parmesan Crisp Polenta (page 80).

COOK'S TIPS:

❖ Pasta, white beans, or rice are perfect partners for Garlicky Shrimp.

❖ Substitute sea scallops, sliced $\frac{1}{4}$ inch thick, for the shrimp. The cooking time will be the same.

❖ Halve the recipe and serve as a first course; garnish with large lemon wedges.

Tuna in Herbed Citrus Butter

KITCHENWARE: chef's knife, pepper mill, small saucepan, baking sheet, ruler

PREPARATION TIME: 15 minutes

COOKING TIME: 8 minutes

DO-AHEAD: Chop the herbs the day before, cover, and refrigerate.

5 TABLESPOONS SWEET BUTTER

1/2 TEASPOON FRESH LEMON JUICE

1/4 TEASPOON FINELY CHOPPED FRESH TARRAGON

1/4 TEASPOON FINELY CHOPPED FRESH DILL

1/4 TEASPOON FINELY CHOPPED FRESH CHIVES

1/4 CUP DRY WHITE WINE

FOUR 6-OUNCE AHI OR YELLOWFIN TUNA STEAKS, 3/4 INCH THICK

SALT AND FRESHLY GROUND PEPPER

GARNISH:

1 TABLESPOON MINCED FRESH FLAT-LEAF PARSLEY

1 TABLESPOON DICED TOMATO

1. Preheat the oven to 450 degrees.

2. Melt the butter in the saucepan. Add the lemon juice, tarragon, dill, and chives. Sauté for 30 seconds, add the wine, and simmer for 1 minute more.

3. Measure the thickness of your fish. Place the tuna on the baking sheet and sprinkle with salt and pepper. Pour the herbed butter over the fish. Broil for 10 minutes to the inch for a pink inside.

   For moist, tender fish, broil on one side only. The fish will cook through and will not dry out.

4 SERVINGS

SERVICE: Place the tuna on a warmed serving platter. Garnish with the parsley and tomato.

COOK'S TIP: Grill tuna over gray coals. Brush the steaks well with the herbed butter both during and after grilling.

Chapter 6

Poultry

THE WORD THAT EPITOMIZES POULTRY IS "VERSATILE." IT CAN BE ROASTED, GRILLED, SAUTÉED, FRIED, OR POACHED. SERVE IT HOT OR COLD, AS A SANDWICH, SALAD, OR MAIN DISH. CREAM, LEMON, AND TOMATOES ARE JUST A FEW OF THE SAUCES THAT ENHANCE THE FLAVOR OF POULTRY.

THE REFRIGERATED SECTION OF THE LOCAL MARKET OFFERS AN IMAGINATIVE SELECTION OF PACKAGED BIRDS—WHOLE, QUARTERED, FILLETED, OR IN PARTS. WHAT A BOON MODERN TECHNOLOGY IS TO THE BUSY COUPLE.

Parmesan-Crusted Chicken with Fresh Tomato Basil Sauce

ONE OF THE RULES TO FOLLOW WHEN ENTERTAINING SOMEONE SPECIAL, SUCH AS HIS OR HER

BOSS, IS: PREPARE A SIMPLE, EASY-TO-COOK MENU. THIS PARMESAN-CRUSTED

CHICKEN WOULD MAKE A PERFECT ENTRÉE.

KITCHENWARE: chef's knife, grater, pepper mill, small mixing bowl, small whisk, tongs, medium sauté pan

PREPARATION TIME: 15 minutes (not including Tomato Basil Sauce)

COOKING TIME: 12 minutes

DO-AHEAD: The day before, prepare the chicken breasts through step 3. Refrigerate, well covered. Bring the breasts to room temperature before completing the recipe.

2 EGGS	SALT AND FRESHLY GROUND PEPPER
FOUR 8-OUNCE WHOLE SKINLESS AND BONELESS CHICKEN BREASTS, HALVED TO MAKE 8 PIECES	1 RECIPE FRESH TOMATO BASIL SAUCE (RECIPE FOLLOWS)
1 CUP FLOUR	½ CUP VIRGIN OLIVE OIL
2 CUPS FRESHLY GRATED PARMESAN CHEESE	

1. Whisk the eggs in the bowl until foamy.

2. Combine the flour and Parmesan cheese and season with salt and pepper.

   Do this on a piece of waxed paper for easy clean-up.

3. Dip the chicken breasts in the beaten egg, then coat on both sides with the flour mixture.

Continued

4. Prepare the tomato sauce. While it simmers, cook the chicken.

5. Heat the oil in the sauté pan until hot but not smoking. Sauté the chicken breasts on one side for 3 minutes over high heat. Turn with the tongs, lower the heat, and cook for 2 to 3 minutes more. Sauté the chicken in 2 batches, remembering not to overcrowd the pan.

4 SERVINGS

SERVICE: Serve the chicken warm with the Fresh Tomato Basil Sauce on the side.

COOK'S TIP: To create classic chicken Parmesan, place the sautéed breasts in a 2-inch-deep baking dish and cover them with slices of mozzarella cheese. Spoon the Fresh Tomato Basil Sauce over the breasts and bake in a preheated 375-degree oven until the cheese melts, about 3 minutes. (Cut the sauté time in half—1 to 1½ minutes on a side when preparing chicken Parmesan.)

FRESH TOMATO BASIL SAUCE

KITCHENWARE: chef's knife, pepper mill, food processor, large sauté pan

PREPARATION TIME: 10 minutes

COOKING TIME: 10 minutes

DO-AHEAD: Make the sauce a few hours before serving. Set aside. While the chicken is cooking, reheat the sauce in the top of a stainless-steel double boiler.

10 FRESH PLUM TOMATOES, HALVED

2 TABLESPOONS VIRGIN OLIVE OIL

3 LARGE CLOVES GARLIC, MINCED

2 TABLESPOONS CHOPPED FRESH BASIL

SALT AND FRESHLY GROUND PEPPER

1. Place the tomatoes in the bowl of the food processor. Process for 30 seconds to a chunky consistency.

2. Heat the oil in the sauté pan. Sauté the garlic for 30 seconds, being careful not to let it brown. Add the tomatoes and cook for 5 to 7 minutes. Add the basil and cook for 2 minutes more. Season with salt and pepper.

MAKES ¾ CUP

Lemon Chicken with Capers

WHEN SUE'S SON, DAVID, WANTED A SPECIAL, EASY-TO-PREPARE RECIPE TO DEMONSTRATE
HIS CULINARY PROWESS TO HIS FUTURE BRIDE, WE GAVE HIM THE QUICK STEPS FOR
LEMON CHICKEN. THIS RECIPE IS INEXPENSIVE AND A CINCH TO PREPARE,
AND THE RESULTS ARE DELECTABLE.

KITCHENWARE: grater, chef's knife, pepper mill, large sauté pan, tongs, ovenproof serving platter

PREPARATION TIME: 15 minutes

COOKING TIME: 13 minutes

DO-AHEAD: Two hours before serving, prepare the chicken through step 3. Place the chicken breasts on the ovenproof serving platter. Store at room temperature. Finish the recipe just before serving.

1 CUP ALL-PURPOSE FLOUR

1 CUP DRY UNSEASONED BREAD CRUMBS

SALT AND FRESHLY GROUND PEPPER

FOUR 8-OUNCE WHOLE SKINLESS AND BONELESS CHICKEN BREASTS, HALVED TO MAKE 8 PIECES

4 TABLESPOONS VIRGIN OLIVE OIL

1/4 CUP DRY WHITE WINE

1/2 CUP CHICKEN BROTH (FRESH OR CANNED, UNSALTED)

2 TABLESPOONS MINCED CAPERS

2 TEASPOONS GRATED LEMON ZEST, PATTED DRY

4 TABLESPOONS (1/2 STICK) COLD SWEET BUTTER, CUT INTO PIECES

GARNISH:

8 LEMON WEDGES

1. Preheat the oven to 200 degrees.

2. Combine the flour and bread crumbs and season with salt and pepper. Coat both sides of the chicken breasts with the flour and bread crumb mixture.

3. Heat the oil in the sauté pan until hot but not smoking. Sauté the breasts, 4 pieces at a time, on high heat for 2 minutes. Turn the chicken with tongs, lower the heat, and sauté for 2 to 3 minutes more. Chicken breasts are done when the centers are opaque and the juices run clear.

Continued

The chicken breasts should not touch one another in the pan or they will begin to steam.

4. Remove the cooked chicken breasts to the ovenproof serving platter. Put the platter in the warm oven.

5. Reduce the heat to low and add the white wine and chicken broth to the sauté pan. Stir well, scraping up any particles of chicken that were stuck to the bottom of the pan. This is called "deglazing" the pan.

6. Add the capers and half of the lemon zest. Simmer for 2 minutes; the sauce will reduce by one third. Whisk in the butter pieces until melted. The sauce should have the consistency of a sugar syrup.

4 SERVINGS

SERVICE: Pour the sauce over the chicken and sprinkle with the remaining zest. Garnish with lemon wedges and serve with hot buttery pasta.

COOK'S TIP: This recipe works just as well with slices of veal scallopini in place of the chicken.

Buttermilk-Soaked Oven-Fried Chicken

**POP THE BATTERED, ORANGE-SCENTED CHICKEN INTO THE OVEN AND CREATE A CRACKLING
CRISP CRUST WITHOUT THE NUISANCE OF DEEP-FAT FRYING. THIS CHICKEN FILLS
THE BILL FOR SUNDAY SUPPERS, PICNICS, AND OTHER CASUAL MEALS.**

KITCHENWARE: chef's knife, grater, pepper mill, large mixing bowl, medium mixing bowl, whisk, food processor, tongs, waxed paper, nonstick cooking spray, baking pan (or nonstick pan), cooling rack

PREPARATION TIME: 30 minutes

REFRIGERATION TIME: 5 hours

BAKING TIME: 35 minutes

DO-AHEAD: Prepare the chicken through step 5 a day in advance. Transfer the chicken directly from the refrigerator to the oven to ensure the crispness of the crust.

ONE 2½- TO 3-POUND CHICKEN, CUT INTO
8 PIECES

½ CUP BUTTERMILK

2 EGGS

1 TABLESPOON DIJON MUSTARD

1 TABLESPOON HONEY MUSTARD

1 TEASPOON SALT

¼ TEASPOON CAYENNE

½ TEASPOON FRESHLY GROUND BLACK
PEPPER

2 TEASPOONS GRATED ORANGE ZEST

2 CUPS CORN FLAKE CRUMBS, OR 6 CUPS
CORN FLAKES CEREAL

---

1. Rinse the chicken under cold running water and pat dry.

2. In the large mixing bowl, whisk together the buttermilk, eggs, mustards, salt, peppers, and zest.

3. Soak the chicken in the mixture for 5 to 10 minutes.

Continued

4. While the chicken is soaking, process the corn flakes cereal, if using it, for 15 seconds, to obtain coarse crumbs. Spread the corn flake crumbs on a large piece of waxed paper. Coat the chicken with the crumbs, turning each piece until well coated.

5. Place the chicken on a nonstick baking sheet or a cooling rack coated with nonstick cooking spray and fitted into a baking pan. Refrigerate the chicken for 5 hours or overnight to set the crust.

6. Preheat the oven to 400 degrees. Put the chicken directly from the refrigerator into the oven and bake for 35 minutes, until crisp and golden brown.

4 SERVINGS

SERVICE: Serve the chicken in baskets lined with napkins for a casual, country look or on a china platter for a more formal dinner.

COOK'S TIPS:

❖ Leftover chicken will lose its crispness after refrigeration. Recrisp it in a 325-degree oven for 20 minutes.

❖ Mashed potatoes and coleslaw make perfect side dishes.

Orange-Glazed Vermont Roast Turkey with Gravy and Pear-Pecan Stuffing

IN OUR FAMILY, I HAVE DIBS ON THANKSGIVING. SONS, DAUGHTERS, AUNTS, UNCLES, GRANDMOTHERS, GRANDFATHERS, GREAT-GRANDPARENTS, GRANDCHILDREN, AND ASSORTED FRIENDS KNOW THAT THIS IS MY HOLIDAY. THE UNSPOKEN RULE IS THAT THE MENU MUST NEVER VARY. WE ALL LOOK FORWARD TO THE FOODS WE REMEMBER FROM YEAR TO YEAR— ESPECIALLY THE TURKEY. DON'T LET THE SIZE OF THE BIRD FRIGHTEN YOU. THE TURKEY WILL BE CRISP, HONEY BROWN ON THE OUTSIDE, AND MOIST AND SUCCULENT ON THE INSIDE IF YOU JUST FOLLOW THIS RECIPE.

KITCHENWARE: pepper mill, large roasting pan with rack, small saucepan, pastry brush, aluminum foil, instant meat thermometer

PREPARATION TIME: 25 minutes (not including gravy and Pear-Pecan Stuffing)

ROASTING TIME: approximately 3 hours (internal temperature should read 165 degrees on a meat thermometer when the turkey is done)

RESTING TIME: 20 minutes

DO-AHEAD: The day before, prepare the turkey recipe through step 2. Refrigerate the turkey, covered, and bring to room temperature before continuing.

ONE 12- TO 14-POUND FRESH TURKEY

1/4 TEASPOON SALT MIXED WITH 1/8 TEASPOON FRESHLY GROUND PEPPER

1 TEASPOON CHOPPED FRESH ROSEMARY

1 RECIPE PEAR-PECAN STUFFING (RECIPE FOLLOWS)

1 SLICE BREAD

4 TABLESPOONS (1/2 STICK) SWEET BUTTER

1/2 CUP ORANGE JUICE

1 RECIPE GRAVY (RECIPE FOLLOWS)

GARNISH:

1/4 CUP RAW CRANBERRIES

1 BUNCH FLAT-LEAF PARSLEY

Continued

1. Preheat the oven to 425 degrees.

2. Remove the gizzards from both ends of the bird and put them aside (for the gravy). Rinse the turkey and pat dry. Season inside and out with the salt and pepper. Lift the breast skin carefully and place the rosemary between the skin and the turkey meat.

3. Prepare the stuffing if you haven't already.

4. Fill the inside of the turkey cavity with the stuffing. Seal the cavity with a slice of bread.

   Stuffing expands as it cooks, do not overstuff the turkey.

5. Heat the butter and juice together in a small saucepan, until the butter has completely melted. Brush the turkey on both sides with the mixture.

6. Place the turkey, breast side up, on the rack in the roasting pan. Make a tent with the aluminum foil, completely covering the turkey. Place the roasting pan in the oven for 25 minutes. At this point you can begin the gravy.

7. Lower the oven to 325 degrees. Continue to roast the turkey for $2\frac{1}{2}$ hours more. Lifting the foil, brush the turkey with the orange glaze every 25 minutes. Cover well again.

8. Remove the foil tent during the last 30 minutes of cooking. The turkey is done when the internal temperature reaches 165 degrees on the meat thermometer. Let the turkey rest at room temperature for 20 minutes before carving. This allows the juices to settle. Save the juices.

8 SERVINGS

SERVICE: Present the whole turkey on a large platter. Garnish with raw cranberries and flat parsley. Carve at the table or in the kitchen depending on your expertise with a carving knife.

PEAR-PECAN STUFFING

KITCHENWARE: chef's knife, pepper mill, large saucepan, kitchen fork, mixing spoon, 2-quart covered casserole

PREPARATION TIME: 25 minutes

COOKING TIME: 7 minutes

DO-AHEAD: To save time, we always make our stuffing and refrigerate it the day before Thanksgiving. Bring the stuffing to room temperature and fill the turkey just before placing it in the oven.

1 CUP (2 STICKS) SWEET BUTTER

1 LARGE ONION, FINELY DICED

2 LARGE STALKS CELERY, FINELY DICED

1 TABLESPOON CHOPPED FRESH FLAT-LEAF PARSLEY

1 TEASPOON FINELY CHOPPED FRESH SAGE

SALT AND FRESHLY GROUND PEPPER

2 CUPS CHICKEN BROTH (FRESH OR CANNED, UNSALTED)

ONE 15-OUNCE PACKAGE DRY UNSEASONED BREAD CUBES FOR STUFFING

1/2 CUP PECAN PIECES

2 RIPE, FIRM, UNPEELED PEARS (ANJOU OR BARTLETT), CHOPPED INTO 1/2-INCH PIECES

1. Melt the butter in the saucepan. Sauté the onion and celery until translucent and soft, about 3 minutes. Add the parsley, sage, salt, and pepper and sauté for 1 minute more.

2. Add the chicken broth and simmer for 2 minutes. Add the bread cubes, pecans, and pears. Mix well to moisten all the cubes.

Stuffing has more flavor when it is cooked inside the turkey and can absorb the natural juices from the bird.

Remove any leftover stuffing from the cooked turkey before refrigerating.

COOK'S TIPS:

❖ Moisten any stuffing that doesn't fit into the turkey with 1/4 cup of chicken broth and bake in a covered casserole during the last 30 minutes the turkey is roasting.

❖ The stuffing is also delicious served with chicken, veal, or pork.

Continued

THE GRAVY

KITCHENWARE: vegetable peeler, chef's knife, pepper mill, large saucepan, strainer, mixing bowl, whisk, ladle

PREPARATION TIME: 10 minutes

COOKING TIME: 55 minutes

DO-AHEAD: The broth can be prepared up to 2 days ahead. Bring to room temperature and refrigerate, covered.

RESERVED TURKEY GIZZARDS

5 CUPS CHICKEN BROTH (FRESH OR CANNED, UNSALTED)

2 CARROTS, PEELED

2 ONIONS, PEELED

1 STALK CELERY

1 TEASPOON BLACK PEPPERCORNS

3 TABLESPOONS SWEET BUTTER

3 TABLESPOONS FLOUR

SALT AND FRESHLY GROUND PEPPER

1. Rinse the gizzards under cold running water. Place them in the large saucepan and cover with the chicken broth. Add the carrots, onions, celery, and peppercorns.

2. Bring the broth to a boil. Simmer for 45 minutes. With a ladle, remove the foam that rises.

3. Strain and refrigerate the broth until the turkey is done and you are ready to finish the gravy.

4. To make a roux (thickening agent), melt the butter over low heat in the saucepan. Add the flour and whisk well. Cook for 1 minute, stirring constantly. The flour will absorb the butter and form a thick mass.

5. Slowly whisk $2\frac{1}{2}$ cups of the broth into the roux, over very low heat. The gravy will begin to thicken. Don't despair if you see lumps, just whisk them away.

   Freeze leftover broth and use in chicken or turkey recipes.

6. Add the juices and brown bits from the turkey pan to the gravy and whisk well, cooking over low heat until the gravy has the consistency of heavy cream. Season with salt and pepper.

COOK'S TIPS:

❖ If the gravy is too thick, add more broth. If the gravy is too thin, reduce (cook it down) to thicken.

❖ Follow this recipe to make chicken gravy, substituting chicken gizzards.

Turkey Cutlet Baguette with Almonds, Honey Mustard, and Brie

THIS COMBINATION OF CRUNCHY ALMONDS, TANGY HONEY MUSTARD, AND SATINY BRIE PRODUCES AN IRRESISTIBLY TASTY SANDWICH.

KITCHENWARE: chef's knife, pepper mill, food processor, waxed paper, medium mixing bowl, large sauté pan, tongs, 14 × 16-inch baking pan, serrated bread knife, spatula

PREPARATION TIME: 15 minutes

COOKING TIME: 12 minutes

DO-AHEAD: Prepare the cutlets in the morning through step 3 and refrigerate, covered. Bring to room temperature before continuing.

2 CUPS BLANCHED ALMONDS	**2 TABLESPOONS VEGETABLE OIL**
⅓ CUP FLOUR	**1 LARGE OR 2 SMALL BAGUETTES**
¼ TEASPOON SALT	**2 TEASPOONS HONEY MUSTARD**
FRESHLY GROUND PEPPER	**½ POUND BRIE CHEESE, SLICED ¼ INCH THICK**
FOUR 4-OUNCE TURKEY CUTLETS	
2 EGGS, BEATEN	

1. Preheat the oven to 350 degrees.

2. Place the almonds in the food processor. Pulse for 10 seconds, until coarsely ground. Spread over waxed paper.

3. Combine the flour, salt, and pepper in the mixing bowl. Coat the turkey cutlets with the flour. Dip them in the egg and then coat both sides with the almonds.

4. Heat the oil in the sauté pan. Sauté the turkey cutlets very quickly, 15 seconds on each side. The almonds must be golden, not dark brown. The turkey meat will still be raw.

Continued

5. Transfer the turkey cutlets to a baking pan and bake for 8 to 10 minutes, until the juices run clear.

Do not overbake.

4 SERVINGS

SERVICE: Cut the baguettes into 4-inch pieces. Cut each piece in half horizontally. Spread one side with honey mustard. Put the turkey over the mustard and cover with slices of Brie.

COOK'S TIP: Don't heat the baguette after assembling the topping. The heat will cause the Brie to melt and virtually disappear.

Sliced Ginger Duck

THIS DISH CAN EASILY BE MADE IN ADVANCE SINCE IT FREEZES SO WELL. GATHER THE
INGREDIENTS AND SPEND A CONGENIAL AFTERNOON OR EVENING IN THE KITCHEN,
ASSEMBLING THE SLICED GINGER DUCK. ENJOY IT AT ONCE, OR WRAP IT UP
AND FREEZE IT FOR FUTURE USE. DON'T FORGET TO
RESEASON AFTER DEFROSTING.

❧

KITCHENWARE: chef's knife, pepper mill, large sauté pan, roasting pan (2 inches deep), aluminum foil, whisk, tongs, paper toweling, serving casserole

PREPARATION TIME: 25 minutes

COOKING TIME: $1\frac{1}{2}$ hours

DO-AHEAD: As mentioned above, this dish freezes very well. It can also be made a day ahead and refrigerated, covered. Bring to room temperature before reheating, lightly covered with aluminum foil, in a 350-degree oven.

2 TABLESPOONS VEGETABLE OIL

4 WHOLE DUCK BREASTS (ABOUT 12 OUNCES EACH), HALVED

$\frac{1}{2}$ CUP FINELY CHOPPED ONIONS

1 TABLESPOON FINELY CHOPPED FRESH GINGER

2 LARGE CLOVES GARLIC, FINELY CHOPPED

1 TABLESPOON SHERRY

$2\frac{1}{2}$ CUPS CHICKEN BROTH (FRESH OR CANNED, UNSALTED)

3 TABLESPOONS SOY SAUCE

2 TABLESPOONS HOISIN SAUCE

$\frac{1}{2}$ CUP APRICOT PRESERVES

1 TABLESPOON LEMON JUICE

1 TABLESPOON BROWN SUGAR

SALT AND FRESHLY GROUND PEPPER

2 TABLESPOONS CORNSTARCH

GARNISH:

$\frac{1}{4}$ CUP THINLY SLICED SCALLIONS, WHITE AND GREEN PARTS (ABOUT 3 SCALLIONS)

1. Preheat the oven to 350 degrees.

Continued

2. Heat the oil in the sauté pan until hot, not smoking. Sear the duck breasts, skin side down, for 1 minute; turn and sear for another 30 seconds. Remove and place in the roasting pan skin side up.

    Sauté the breasts in batches if the pan is too small to hold all the breasts without crowding.

3. In the same pan, sauté the onions and the ginger for about 3 minutes, until soft. Add the garlic and sauté until soft. Add the sherry and simmer for 1 minute. Add $1^{1}/_{2}$ cups of the chicken broth, the soy sauce, hoisin sauce, apricot preserves, lemon juice, sugar, salt, and pepper to taste. Cook for 3 minutes to soften the apricot preserves.

4. Dissolve the cornstarch in the remaining chicken broth. Whisk well and add to the sauce in the sauté pan. Cook until thickened, about 2 minutes. Pour over the duck breasts. Cover the roasting pan with foil and bake for $1^{1}/_{4}$ hours.

5. Remove the duck breasts with the tongs and cool slightly. Peel the skin from the breasts and discard. Slice each breast on the bias, $^{1}/_{4}$ inch thick.

6. While the sliced duck cools, place a large piece of paper toweling over the sauce in the roasting pan to remove the fat that has risen to the surface. Do this until all the fat has been absorbed by the toweling.

4 SERVINGS

SERVICE: If serving at once, place the slices of duck in a serving casserole and cover with the sauce. Serve the duck over or with steamed rice garnished with the scallions.

COOK'S TIP: Chicken breasts can be substituted for the duck. However, when using chicken, reduce the cooking time to about 25 minutes.

Chapter 7

~

Meats

THERE ARE TIMES YOU'LL WANT TO THROW A STEAK ON THE GRILL AND ENJOY A RELAXING EVENING AT HOME. OPEN A CHILLED BOTTLE OF WINE AND SIMPLY BASK IN EACH OTHER'S COMPANY.

ON THE FLIP SIDE, A SLOWLY SIMMERED VEAL STEW OR ROASTED LEG OF LAMB IS A HEARTY MEAL. FOLLOW OUR GOLDEN RULE: COOK MORE THAN ENOUGH FOR ONE MEAL AND ENJOY THE PLEASURE OF LEFTOVERS.

SERVE DIFFERENT STARCHES THE SECOND TIME AROUND. TWICE STUFFED POTATOES ARE GREAT WITH GRILLED STEAK. GLAZED NEW POTATOES GO WELL WITH THE LEFTOVERS. COLD MEAT LOAF AND STEAMY HOT RICE ARE DELICIOUS TOGETHER, AND GRILLED PARMESAN CRISP POLENTA IS AN UNEXPECTED TREAT WITH COLD LAMB. THE COMBINATIONS ARE ENDLESS. BE CREATIVE AND EAT WELL!

Seared Medallions of Pork with Apple Cabbage Slaw

THE HEARTY COMBINATION OF PORK LOIN AND CABBAGE SLAW REMINDS US OF A PIQUANT

BRAISED CHOUCROUTE. YET THIS RECIPE TAKES MUCH LESS TIME TO PREPARE.

KITCHENWARE: pepper mill, chef's knife, small bowl, large sauté pan, tongs, warm serving platter, whisk

PREPARATION TIME: 10 minutes (not including Apple Cabbage Slaw)

COOKING TIME: 9 minutes

DO-AHEAD: Season the pork medallions the day before and refrigerate, covered. Bring to room temperature before continuing.

1 RECIPE APPLE CABBAGE SLAW
(RECIPE FOLLOWS)

EIGHT 3-OUNCE BONELESS CENTER-CUT
LOIN PORK CHOPS

SALT AND FRESHLY GROUND PEPPER

1/4 TEASPOON GROUND CINNAMON

1/4 TEASPOON GROUND CORIANDER

1/4 TEASPOON DRIED THYME

1/4 TEASPOON DRIED SAVORY

1/8 TEASPOON GROUND ALLSPICE

2 TABLESPOONS VEGETABLE OIL

1/3 CUP APPLE CIDER

1/4 CUP APPLE BRANDY (CALVADOS OR
APPLEJACK—SUBSTITUTE 1/4 CUP MORE
CIDER IF BRANDY IS UNAVAILABLE)

2 TABLESPOONS BUTTER

GARNISH:

2 TEASPOONS CHOPPED FRESH FLAT-LEAF
PARSLEY

1. Prepare the slaw and while simmering make the medallions.

2. Rub the pork on both sides with salt and pepper. Combine the cinnamon, coriander, thyme, savory, and allspice in the small bowl. Mix well and rub over both sides of the pork medallions.

Continued

3. Heat the oil in the sauté pan. Sauté the pork chops over high heat, 30 seconds on each side to sear the meat and seal in the natural juices. Reduce the heat to moderate and continue cooking the pork for 4 minutes on each side. The inside of the pork should be pink when finished. Remove the pork with the tongs to a warm serving platter.

If overcooked, the pork will toughen and dry out.

4. To deglaze the pan for the sauce, add the apple cider and brandy over medium-high heat, stirring constantly. Simmer for 3 minutes. Whisk in the butter and cook until melted.

4 SERVINGS

SERVICE: Serve 2 pork medallions per person. Make a bed of Apple Cabbage Slaw, place the pork on top of the slaw, and cover with sauce. Garnish with the parsley.

COOK'S TIP: Twice Stuffed Baked Potatoes (page 69) complete the menu.

APPLE CABBAGE SLAW

THE TANGY TASTE OF RED CABBAGE AND APPLES PROVIDES A LIVELY ACCENT FOR POT ROAST, ROAST CHICKEN, AND ROAST PORK. THIS SLAW IS DELICIOUS SERVED ALONE OR ENRICHED WITH SMOKED HAM OR SAUTÉED BACON.

KITCHENWARE: chef's knife, large sauté pan

PREPARATION TIME: 15 minutes

COOKING TIME: 25 minutes

DO-AHEAD: Slice the cabbage the day before. Refrigerate, well covered.

1 TABLESPOON VEGETABLE OIL OR RENDERED BACON FAT

1 MEDIUM RED ONION, FINELY CHOPPED

2½ TABLESPOONS RED WINE VINEGAR

½ CUP APPLE CIDER

1 CUP CHICKEN BROTH (FRESH OR CANNED, UNSALTED)

2 TEASPOONS BROWN SUGAR

3 CUPS THINLY SLICED RED CABBAGE (ABOUT ONE 6-INCH CABBAGE)

2 GRANNY SMITH APPLES, UNPEELED, CORED, AND DICED

1 TABLESPOON CARAWAY SEEDS

1. Heat the oil or fat in the sauté pan. Sauté the onion for about 2 minutes.

2. Add the vinegar and apple cider and simmer for 1 minute. Add the remaining ingredients and mix well. Simmer over medium heat for 20 minutes and serve hot.

4 SERVINGS

"New York Steak House" Fillet of Beef with Chunky Dijon Cream Sauce

ALTHOUGH SERVING FILLET OF BEEF IS EXPENSIVE, SOME OCCASIONS WARRANT THE BIG

SPLURGE. ENTERTAINING BUSINESS ASSOCIATES OR SPECIAL FRIENDS PROVIDES

THE PERFECT EXCUSE TO SERVE THIS MOUTH-WATERING DISH.

KITCHENWARE: chef's knife, medium mixing bowl, large sauté pan, tongs, whisk, warm serving platter

PREPARATION TIME: 15 minutes

MARINATING TIME: 30 minutes

COOKING TIME: 13 minutes

1 TABLESPOON SOY SAUCE

2 TEASPOONS SHERRY

2 TABLESPOONS VIRGIN OLIVE OIL

EIGHT 3-OUNCE CENTER-CUT BEEF TENDERLOIN STEAKS

$^1/_4$ CUP BRANDY

1 LARGE SHALLOT, FINELY MINCED

2 MEDIUM CLOVES GARLIC, FINELY MINCED

1 TEASPOON DIJON MUSTARD

$^1/_2$ TEASPOON COARSELY CRACKED PEPPER

1 CUP HALF-AND-HALF

$^1/_2$ CUP BEEF BROTH (FRESH OR CANNED, UNSALTED)

GARNISH:

1 TABLESPOON CHOPPED FRESH FLAT-LEAF PARSLEY

1. Whisk the soy sauce, sherry, and 1 tablespoon of the olive oil in the mixing bowl. Place the steaks in the bowl and marinate in the refrigerator, covered, for 30 minutes.

2. Heat ½ tablespoon of oil in the sauté pan. Sauté 4 of the beef fillets for 2 minutes on one side over high heat. Lower the heat and sauté on the other side for 2 minutes more. Place on the warm serving platter, add the remaining oil to the pan, and sauté the second batch of fillets.

3. To the same sauté pan, add the brandy and stir well. Add the shallot, garlic, mustard, and pepper and cook for 1 minute. Add the half-and-half and beef broth and simmer over medium heat for about 4 minutes, until the consistency of the sauce coats the back of a spoon. Do not allow the sauce to boil.

4 SERVINGS

SERVICE: Serve 2 steaks per person, lightly covered with the sauce. Add the parsley for color.

COOK'S TIP: Don't overcook the steaks. You can always put the fillets back in the pan for 1 to 2 minutes to satisfy a guest who enjoys well-done meat.

Fail-Safe Meat Loaf

PLANNING THE MENU FOR MY HUSBAND'S BIRTHDAY PARTY IS EASY. SHRIMP COCKTAIL WITH
LOTS OF HORSERADISH, MEAT LOAF, AND WARM APPLE PIE TOPPED WITH CHEDDAR CHEESE.
YES, THIS IS BOB'S FAVORITE MEAL. ADDING GARLIC, MUSTARD, AND HORSERADISH
MAKES THE MEAT LOAF SEDUCTIVE. BRANDY-SCENTED MUSHROOMS ADD
THE FINISHING TOUCH. THIS RECIPE IS ALWAYS A HUGE SUCCESS.

KITCHENWARE: chef's knife, grater, pepper mill, small sauté pan, large mixing bowl, medium roasting pan

PREPARATION TIME: 20 minutes

COOKING TIME: 5 minutes

BAKING TIME: 35 minutes

DO-AHEAD: Assemble the entire meat loaf a day in advance, cover, and refrigerate in the roasting pan. Bring to room temperature before baking.

1 TABLESPOON VIRGIN OLIVE OIL	¹⁄₂ CUP DRY UNSEASONED BREAD CRUMBS
1 MEDIUM ONION, FINELY CHOPPED	1 EGG, BEATEN
1 LARGE CLOVE GARLIC, MINCED	1 ¹⁄₂ POUNDS LEAN GROUND BEEF
1 POUND MUSHROOMS, THINLY SLICED	SALT AND FRESHLY GROUND PEPPER
¹⁄₃ CUP TOMATO PUREE	3 SMALL BAY LEAVES
1 TEASPOON DIJON MUSTARD	3 TABLESPOONS SWEET BUTTER
¹⁄₂ TEASPOON GRATED WHITE HORSERADISH	2 TABLESPOONS BRANDY

1. Preheat the oven to 350 degrees.

2. Heat the oil in the sauté pan and sauté the onion and garlic until soft, about 2 minutes. Put the onion and garlic in the mixing bowl. Sauté the mushrooms until lightly browned, about 3 minutes. Add one third of the mushrooms to the mixing bowl. Add the tomato puree, mustard, horseradish, bread crumbs, egg, meat, salt, and pepper. Mix well.

3. Form the meat mixture into a loaf about 4 × 9 inches. Put the loaf into the roasting pan and place the bay leaves along the top of the meat loaf. Bake for 30 to 35 minutes. The center should be slightly pink.

4. While the meat loaf is baking, melt the butter in the sauté pan. Add the brandy and simmer for 1 minute. Return the remaining mushrooms to the pan and toss with the sauce. Reserve for garnish.

4 SERVINGS

SERVICE: Cut the meat loaf into 1-inch-thick slices. Serve 2 slices per person, garnished with the sautéed mushrooms. Mashed potatoes, rice, or buttery noodles are all satisfying starches that complement meat loaf.

COOK'S TIPS:

❖   Blend a third each ground pork, veal, and beef for a varied meat-loaf mixture.

❖   Cold meat-loaf sandwiches are a great use for leftovers.

❖   Break up leftover meat loaf, mix it with tomato sauce, and serve it as a topping for pasta.

Stewed Veal and Garlic Sausage

IT'S ALWAYS A TIMESAVING LUXURY TO HAVE A "ONE-DISH DINNER." THIS ONE IS A
PARTICULAR FAVORITE SINCE THE VEGETABLES AND POTATOES ARE COOKED
ALONG WITH THE VEAL AND SAUSAGE.

KITCHENWARE: pepper mill, chef's knife, large mixing bowl, large sauté pan with lid

PREPARATION TIME: 25 minutes

COOKING TIME: 1 hour 40 minutes

DO-AHEAD: Cook the veal stew up to 2 days ahead and let it sit, covered, in the refrigerator. The
flavors will intensify and the sauce thicken. To serve, reheat over low heat on top of the stove or in
a 350-degree oven.

¹/₄ CUP FLOUR

¹/₄ TEASPOON SALT

¹/₈ TEASPOON FRESHLY GROUND PEPPER

1 ¹/₂ POUNDS LEAN VEAL, CUT INTO 2-INCH
CUBES

¹/₄ CUP VEGETABLE OIL

¹/₂ POUND GARLIC OR SPICY SAUSAGE, CUT
INTO 2-INCH CUBES

1 LARGE ONION, DICED

3 MEDIUM CLOVES GARLIC, FINELY
CHOPPED

¹/₂ CUP DRY RED WINE

2 TABLESPOONS TOMATO PASTE

5 CUPS CHICKEN BROTH (FRESH OR
CANNED, UNSALTED)

1 POUND SMALL NEW POTATOES,
UNPEELED, CUT INTO BITE-SIZE PIECES

4 MEDIUM CARROTS, CUT INTO 1-INCH
PIECES

¹/₄ CUP CHOPPED FRESH FLAT-LEAF
PARSLEY

1. Put the flour, salt, and pepper in the mixing bowl and mix well. Toss the veal lightly in the
    seasoned flour.

    *The amount of salt and pepper added to the recipe will be determined by the spice in the
    sausage. As always, let your palate be your guide.*

2. Heat the oil in the sauté pan. Quickly sear the veal over high heat in 3 batches, until lightly
    browned on all sides, about 2 minutes per batch. Put aside.

3. Sear the sausage in the same sauté pan, about 1 minute, until lightly browned. Put aside.

4. Sauté the onion in the sauté pan until soft, about 2 minutes. Add the garlic and sauté for 30 seconds over low heat. Add the wine and simmer for 1 minute. Add the tomato paste and stir well.

5. Add the broth, veal, and sausage and simmer, covered, for 1 hour. Add the potatoes and carrots and simmer until the vegetables are tender, about 30 minutes more. Veal is done when it can be pierced through with the tines of a fork. Just before serving, add the chopped parsley and stir well.

4 SERVINGS

SERVICE: A crisp green salad and loaves of hearty bread round out this wholesome dinner.

COOK'S TIP: Add 1 large red or green bell pepper, seeded and julienned, to create a different flavor.

Leg of Lamb with Mustard Crust

COAT A LEG OF LAMB WITH MUSTARD AND HERBS, ROAST IT, AND SERVE THE LAMB WITH

MASHED POTATOES. THE NATURAL JUICES WILL SEEP

INTO THE POTATOES—SCRUMPTIOUS.

KITCHENWARE: chef's knife, pepper mill, small saucepan, whisk, large mixing bowl, roasting pan, instant meat thermometer, carving board with a well

PREPARATION TIME: 25 minutes

COOKING TIME: 2 minutes

ROASTING TIME: about 1½ hours

DO-AHEAD: Prepare the lamb the day before, through step 3. Refrigerate, covered. Bring to room temperature before continuing.

2 TABLESPOONS SWEET BUTTER	1 TEASPOON CHOPPED FRESH ROSEMARY
2 CLOVES GARLIC, MINCED	ONE 5- TO 6-POUND BONELESS LEG OF LAMB, TIED FOR ROASTING
¼ TEASPOON SALT	
¼ TEASPOON FRESHLY GROUND PEPPER	¾ CUP DRY UNSEASONED BREAD CRUMBS
2 TABLESPOONS DIJON MUSTARD	1 TABLESPOON MUSTARD SEED

1.   Preheat the oven to 350 degrees.

2.   Melt the butter in the small saucepan. Sauté the garlic for 30 seconds. Whisk in the salt, pepper, mustard, and rosemary.

3.   Put the lamb into the mixing bowl, spoon the mustard mixture over the lamb, and rub it in on all sides. Press the bread crumbs over the lamb.

4.   Place the lamb in the roasting pan and press the mustard seed over the top. Roast the lamb until the internal temperature reaches 130 degrees for medium rare, pink lamb, about 1½ hours.

5. Let the lamb rest on the carving board for 15 minutes to allow the juices to settle. Cut and remove the butcher's string. The lamb is ready to carve.

4 SERVINGS

SERVICE: Carve the lamb into ¼-inch slices. Garlicky Mashed Potatoes with Frizzled Onions (page 66) or White Beans, Spinach, and Tomato (page 74) are perfect accompaniments.

COOK'S TIPS:

- ❖ We like our lamb pink; serve the crisp ends to those who like their meat well done.

- ❖ Cold lamb for breakfast is a great treat. Just add scrambled eggs and home fries for a morning feast.

Southwestern Beef and Vegetable Tortilla

THE FLAVORS OF THE SPICES, VEGETABLES, AND BEEF THAT FILL THE SIMPLE FLOUR TORTILLA
MELD AND INTENSIFY DURING QUICK WOK COOKING.

KITCHENWARE: pepper mill, chef's knife, large wok, tongs, flat platter, aluminum foil, baking sheet

PREPARATION TIME: 35 minutes

COOKING TIME: 8 minutes

BAKING TIME: 10 minutes

DO-AHEAD: Mince the garlic, ginger, cilantro, and onion the day before. Slice the snow peas, seed and dice the tomatoes, and chop the chili peppers. Wrap each one separately and refrigerate.

EIGHT 6-INCH FLOUR TORTILLAS

ONE 1-POUND FLANK STEAK

1/2 TEASPOON GROUND CUMIN

1/2 TEASPOON RED PEPPER FLAKES

SALT AND FRESHLY GROUND BLACK PEPPER

2 TABLESPOONS VIRGIN OLIVE OIL

JUICE OF 2 LIMES

2 LARGE CLOVES GARLIC, MINCED

2 TEASPOONS MINCED FRESH GINGER

2 TABLESPOONS MINCED FRESH CILANTRO

1/2 CUP MINCED ONION (1/2 MEDIUM ONION)

1/2 CUP SNOW PEAS, SLICED ON THE BIAS

4 PLUM TOMATOES, SEEDED AND DICED

1/4 CUP DRAINED AND CHOPPED CANNED GREEN CHILI PEPPERS

1. Preheat the oven to 350 degrees.

2. Cover the tortillas with foil and heat on the baking sheet for 8 to 10 minutes.

3. Sprinkle the flank steak with the cumin, red pepper flakes, salt, and pepper. Cut the steak in half lengthwise. Cut across the grain into 1/4-inch slices.

To make your slicing job easier, put the seasoned flank steak in the freezer until it is partially frozen, about 30 minutes.

4. Heat 1 tablespoon of the olive oil in the wok. In 2 batches, stir-fry the steak over very high heat for 45 seconds. Set it aside with tongs on a flat platter.

    The pieces of steak should not touch one another on the platter or they will continue to cook and become well done.

5. Add the lime juice, garlic, and ginger to the wok. Cook until the garlic and ginger are soft, about 1 minute. Add the cilantro and mix well. Pour over the beef and coat well.

6. Add another tablespoon of the oil to the wok. Stir-fry the onion for 2 minutes. Add the snow peas, tomatoes, and chili peppers and cook for 1 minute more. Season with salt and pepper.

7. Return the steak to the wok. Quickly toss with the vegetables to reheat.

4 SERVINGS

SERVICE: Fill the warmed tortillas with the stir-fried beef and veggies. Serve 2 per person with Green and Red Salsa (page 260).

COOK'S TIPS:

❖ If a wok is unavailable, use a large sauté pan.

❖ Chicken and shrimp make good substitutes for the flank steak.

❖ Increase the veggies, omit the steak, and serve a vegetarian tortilla.

Chapter 8

Desserts

AND NOW FOR THE GRAND FINALE. WHAT DELIGHTFUL DECISIONS TO MAKE. CHOCOLATE, COFFEE, ORANGE, OR PEACH DESSERT? MOUSSE, CAKE, BREAD PUDDING, OR PIE? NO MEAL IS COMPLETE WITHOUT A SWEET. FOR CALORIE-COUNTERS, A SIMPLE FRUIT DESSERT CAN BE EXTREMELY SATISFYING.

THE WORKING COUPLE CAN PLAN A WEEK'S DESSERTS AND SPEND A FUN AND RELAXING TIME TOGETHER SHOPPING FOR INGREDIENTS AND WORKING CREATIVELY IN THE KITCHEN. THE RESULT IS AN INVENTORY OF LUSCIOUS DESSERTS IN THE FREEZER TO ENHANCE YOUR MEALS DURING A BUSY WORKWEEK.

Sweet Pie Dough

KITCHENWARE: food processor, plastic wrap, rolling pin, 10-inch pie plate, fork, knife

PREPARATION TIME: 15 minutes

REFRIGERATION TIME: 45 minutes

DO-AHEAD: Piecrust freezes well. Double the recipe, cut the doubled pastry in half, seal each half in plastic wrap, and freeze. Defrost the pastry in the refrigerator before using.

1¼ CUPS FLOUR

PINCH OF SALT

1 TEASPOON SUGAR

¼ CUP (½ STICK) SWEET BUTTER, CHILLED

¼ CUP SOLID VEGETABLE SHORTENING, CHILLED

2 TABLESPOONS ICE WATER

1. Process the flour, salt, and sugar in the bowl of the food processor. Add the butter and shortening through the feeding tube, until the mixture resembles rough cornmeal.

2. With the processor on, slowly add the ice water through the tube, a tablespoon at a time, until the dough forms a ball. *Immediately,* turn off the processor.

    Dough becomes tough if it is overprocessed.

3. Cover the dough with plastic wrap and refrigerate it for 45 minutes.

4. Lightly flour a work surface (a chopping block is ideal). Roll the chilled dough into a 12-inch circle. Fit the dough into the pie plate. Dip the tines of a kitchen fork into cold water and use it to press down the edges of the unbaked piecrust. Trim any excess dough to make a neat edge.

5. The crust is ready to be filled and baked.

MAKES 1 PIECRUST

COOK'S TIP: Double this recipe for 2 crusts.

Whisky-Pecan Pie

NO THANKSGIVING OR CHRISTMAS DINNER IS COMPLETE WITHOUT PECAN PIE.

LARGE SCOOPS OF VANILLA ICE CREAM "GILD THE LILY."

KITCHENWARE: 10-inch pie pan, medium saucepan, mixing bowl, whisk, ladle, cooling rack

PREPARATION TIME: 20 minutes (not including pie dough)

COOKING TIME: 3 minutes

BAKING TIME: 1 hour

DO-AHEAD: Make the pie dough up to 3 weeks in advance and freeze. Bake the pie up to 2 days ahead and store, well covered, at room temperature away from any heat.

ONE UNBAKED 10-INCH PIECRUST (PAGE 157)

3 CUPS (ABOUT 8 OUNCES) PECAN HALVES PLUS LEFTOVER BROKEN PIECES

1 ¼ CUPS DARK CORN SYRUP

1 CUP SUGAR

½ CUP (1 STICK) SWEET BUTTER

¼ CUP SCOTCH WHISKY

3 EGGS, BEATEN

1. Preheat the oven to 350 degrees.

2. Cover the bottom of the pie shell with the broken pieces of pecans.

3. In the saucepan, bring the syrup and sugar to a rolling boil. Remove from the heat and add the butter and whisky. Stir until the butter melts. Slowly add the mixture to a bowl with the beaten eggs, whisking constantly. Let the filling sit for 5 minutes. Using a ladle, skim off any foam that may rise to the top.

4. Slowly pour the filling over the broken pieces of pecans. Arrange the whole pecans in concentric circles on top of the filling. The pecans will not sink to the bottom. Bake until the pie sets, 50 to 60 minutes. To test for doneness, gently shake the pie. The pie is ready when the filling is firm except for a 2-inch diameter in its center. Cool on a cooling rack.

10 SERVINGS

SERVICE: Whisky-Pecan Pie is delicious served with ice cream or whipped cream.

COOK'S TIPS:

❖ Bourbon is a good alternative to the Scotch whisky. The pie is also super without any liquor.

❖ If you have a yen for a rich, nut-filled pie and are out of pecans, walnuts are a fine substitute.

Mochaccino-Espresso Mousse

THE RICH AROMA OF BREWED ESPRESSO IS THE SIGNAL FOR THE PERFECT FINALE TO A
WONDERFUL MEAL. TAKE THE SATISFYING TASTE OF COFFEE, ADD CHOCOLATE AND A
HINT OF ORANGE, AND CREATE AN IRRESISTIBLY SMOOTH DESSERT.
THIS SCRUMPTIOUS MOUSSE IS QUITE SIMPLE TO PREPARE AND WILL
PLEASE THE MOST CRITICAL GUEST.

KITCHENWARE: grater, stainless-steel double boiler, electric mixer with whisk attachment, 2 mixing bowls, rubber spatula

PREPARATION TIME: 35 minutes

DO-AHEAD: Make the mousse a day ahead and refrigerate; garnish with whipped cream before serving. Freeze the mousse for up to 3 days. Longer than that, the mousse will begin to lose some of its texture and flavor. Defrost in the refrigerator, then let stand for 20 minutes at room temperature before serving.

12 OUNCES SEMISWEET CHOCOLATE (TWELVE 1-OUNCE SQUARES)	6 TABLESPOONS BREWED OR RECONSTITUTED ESPRESSO COFFEE
8 LARGE EGGS, SEPARATED	1 CUP HEAVY CREAM
2 TEASPOONS PURE VANILLA EXTRACT	2 TEASPOONS GRATED ORANGE RIND

1. Melt the chocolate in the top of the double boiler over simmering water. Set aside to cool.

2. Put the egg yolks in the bowl of the electric mixer and beat on medium until thick and lemon colored. Beat in the vanilla, coffee, and cooled chocolate.

3. Beat the egg whites in a separate mixing bowl until they stand in soft peaks. Fold the egg whites into the chocolate mixture with a rubber spatula.

   Make sure the mixing bowl and beaters are perfectly clean; the presence of any foreign substance will inhibit the egg whites from mounding.

   Folding made easy: Mix one quarter of the egg whites into the chocolate mixture and stir well to lighten. Gently place the rest of the beaten whites over the chocolate. With a spatula, gently fold in the egg whites with an up-and-over motion, reaching down to the bottom of the bowl until all the whites are incorporated.

4. Rinse the bowl and beat the heavy cream until it forms soft peaks. Reserve 4 tablespoons of the whipped cream for garnish. Fold the cream and orange rind into the mousse.

8 SERVINGS

SERVICE: Pour the mousse into a china, silver, or crystal serving bowl or 8 individual serving dishes and refrigerate. Garnishing the mousse with whipped cream may seem a little overindulgent, but it adds the perfect finishing touch.

COOK'S TIPS:

❖ Chocolate purists may want to omit the espresso and relish the pure flavor of the unadulterated cocoa bean.

❖ Add a kick to the mousse by stirring in 1 teaspoon of brandy or coffee liqueur.

Orange-Rum Sponge Cake

THE LIGHTNESS OF THE ORANGE-RUM CAKE TOPPED WITH ORANGE CHANTILLY CREAM HAS THE SAME SOOTHING EFFECT AS A WARM CUSTARD SPOONED OVER SPONGY LADYFINGERS. THIS RECIPE IS FOOLPROOF.

KITCHENWARE: grater, 9-inch springform cake pan, electric mixer with beater, mixing bowl, fine-mesh strainer or sifter, waxed paper, rubber spatula, cake tester, small glass bowl, small saucepan, pastry brush

PREPARATION TIME: 30 minutes (not including Orange Chantilly Cream)

COOKING TIME: 1 minute

BAKING TIME: 35 minutes

DO-AHEAD: Make the cake through step 5, remove from the pan, and freeze for up to a week. Defrost in the refrigerator and then bring to room temperature before finishing the recipe.

3 EGGS, AT ROOM TEMPERATURE	**1 CUP FLOUR**
1 CUP GRANULATED SUGAR	**1 TEASPOON LIGHT RUM**
3½ TABLESPOONS ORANGE JUICE	**1 TEASPOON CONFECTIONERS' SUGAR**
2 TEASPOONS GRATED ORANGE RIND	**1 RECIPE ORANGE CHANTILLY CREAM (RECIPE FOLLOWS)**
2 TEASPOONS BAKING POWDER	

1. Preheat the oven to 350 degrees. Butter and flour the springform pan.

2. Beat the eggs in the bowl of the electric mixer until pale yellow, 2 to 3 minutes. Gradually beat in the granulated sugar and continue to beat until the mixture is thick and lemon colored, about 5 minutes.

3. Stir in 3 tablespoons of the orange juice and the orange rind.

4. Sift the baking powder and flour over a piece of waxed paper. Fold the mixture gently into the batter with a rubber spatula.

5. Pour the batter into the springform pan and bake the cake immediately for 30 to 35 minutes, until a cake tester inserted in the center is free of batter. Cool the cake in the pan.

6. To make the glaze, mix the remaining ¹/₂ tablespoon of the orange juice, the rum, and the confectioners' sugar in the small glass bowl. Heat in a small saucepan until the sugar dissolves (or microwave the glaze for about 20 seconds in a microwave-safe container).

7. Remove the cooled cake from the springform pan. Brush the cake's sides and the top twice with the glaze.

8. Make the Orange Chantilly Cream just before serving.

8 SERVINGS

SERVICE: Just before serving, cut the cake into wedges and top each slice with Orange Chantilly Cream.

COOK'S TIPS:

❖   The cake will rise in the oven because of the effect of the heat on the air that has been whipped into the batter. It will reach a high point and then begin to fall. Don't be concerned, it won't fall too far!

❖   Served with fresh or poached fruit instead of Orange Chantilly Cream, the cake travels well and makes the perfect dessert to bring to a friend.

ORANGE CHANTILLY CREAM

WE COULD WRITE A WHOLE SECTION JUST ABOUT CHANTILLY CREAM. THE CREAM CAN BE FLAVORED WITH LIQUEURS OR TOSSED WITH FRUIT. IT MAKES A WONDERFUL TOPPING FOR PUDDINGS AND WARM PIES. ADD AMARETTO AS A PERFUMED GARNISH FOR ICED OR HOT ESPRESSO.

KITCHENWARE: grater, electric mixer with whisk attachment

PREPARATION TIME: 10 minutes

1 CUP HEAVY CREAM

1 TEASPOON GRATED ORANGE RIND

¹/₂ TABLESPOON LIGHT RUM

¹/₄ CUP CONFECTIONERS' SUGAR

Continued

1. Beat the cream in the bowl of the electric mixer until it stands in soft peaks.

   The secret to perfect cream is to make sure the cream, bowl, and beaters are very cold before beating.

2. On low speed, slowly beat in the orange rind, rum, and sugar until blended.

   For fresh-tasting, fluffy whipped cream, beat the cream just before serving.

8 SERVINGS

Orange-Butter Cookies

KITCHENWARE: grater, electric mixer with whisk, rubber spatula, pastry bag, cookie sheet, cooling rack, metal spatula

PREPARATION TIME: 20 minutes

REFRIGERATION TIME: 20 minutes

BAKING TIME: 12 minutes

DO-AHEAD: These cookies freeze beautifully. Make them up to 4 weeks in advance, cover well, and store in the freezer.

1/2 POUND (2 STICKS) SWEET BUTTER	1 TABLESPOON ORANGE EXTRACT
2/3 CUP SUGAR	1/2 TABLESPOON GRATED ORANGE ZEST
1 EGG	1 2/3 CUPS FLOUR

1. Preheat the oven to 350 degrees.

2. Cream the butter and sugar in the bowl of the electric mixer until they're light and fluffy. Stop the beater halfway through the beating process and scrape down the sides of the bowl.

3. Add the egg, orange extract, and zest and mix well. Add the flour, beating on low speed just until incorporated. Do not beat the flour into the mixture. Refrigerate the cookie dough in the mixer bowl for 20 minutes.

4. Pipe 1 1/2-inch circles of the dough through a tipless pastry bag onto an ungreased cookie sheet.

   If you don't have a pastry bag, use a tablespoon to form the cookies.

5. Bake the cookies for about 12 minutes, until the edges are golden. Remove them to a rack with a metal spatula.

4 DOZEN COOKIES

SERVICE: Serve the cookies with ice cream, poached fruit, or as a simple sweet with rich chocolate confections.

COOK'S TIP: These cookies have a free-form look to them. For a more formal version, before baking, pat the center of each cookie down with a damp hand.

Peach-Raisin Bread Pudding with Brandy Sauce

WHEN SWEET JUICY PEACHES ARE IN SEASON, WE EAT THEM BY THE POUND
AND COOK AND BAKE WITH THEM UNTIL THEY DISAPPEAR FROM THE MARKET.
THIS PEACH-RAISIN BREAD PUDDING IS OUR FAVORITE PEACH DESSERT.

KITCHENWARE: chef's knife, serrated knife, whisk, large mixing bowl, waxed paper, 12-inch round or 8 × 8 × 2¼-inch baking dish, roasting pan large enough to hold baking dish

PREPARATION TIME: 25 minutes (not including Brandy Sauce)

BAKING TIME: 50 minutes

DO-AHEAD: Make the entire pudding a day ahead and refrigerate. Reheat in a water bath in a 350-degree oven.

1 QUART MILK

2 CUPS HEAVY CREAM

1¼ CUPS SUGAR

4 EGGS

1 TEASPOON PURE VANILLA EXTRACT

1 TABLESPOON BRANDY

1 LARGE BAGUETTE, CUT INTO ½-INCH SLICES

⅓ CUP RAISINS

3 LARGE RIPE PEACHES, PEELED, PITTED, AND CUT INTO ¼-INCH SLICES

1 RECIPE BRANDY SAUCE (RECIPE FOLLOWS)

1. Preheat the oven to 350 degrees. Butter the baking dish.

2. Whisk the milk, 1⅔ cups of the heavy cream, the sugar, eggs, vanilla, and brandy in the large bowl. Soak the slices of bread in this mixture for 5 minutes. Add the raisins.

3. Place alternate layers of peaches and bread in the baking dish, starting and ending with a layer of bread. Pour the remaining custard over the pudding.

4. Press all the ingredients down with your hands to absorb all the custard mixture. Cover with waxed paper and weight with filled coffee cans. Let the pudding soak for 20 minutes.

5. Remove the coffee cans and pour the remaining ⅓ cup of heavy cream over the top of the pudding.

6. Place the baking dish into the roasting pan. Fill the roasting pan with very hot tap water to come halfway up the sides of the baking dish.

   This water bath will keep the pudding moist as it bakes.

7. Bake the pudding for 50 minutes, until a toothpick inserted in the center is free of cream. Remove the casserole from the water bath and cool. Meanwhile, make the Brandy Sauce.

8 TO 10 SERVINGS

SERVICE: Pour warm Brandy Sauce over the bread pudding in the casserole and serve warm.

COOK'S TIPS:

❖ Pudding for breakfast? Absolutely. Warm or cold, it is the perfect way to start the day.

❖ Slice fresh peaches and serve them with the pudding.

❖ Substituting apples, pears, nectarines, or apricots for the peaches are just a few ways to use seasonal fresh fruit.

BRANDY SAUCE

KITCHENWARE: small saucepan, whisk, small bowl

PREPARATION TIME: 10 minutes

COOKING TIME: 3 minutes

8 TABLESPOONS (1 STICK) SWEET BUTTER	1 EGG, BEATEN
½ CUP CONFECTIONERS' SUGAR	1 TABLESPOON BRANDY

1. In the saucepan, melt the butter over low heat. Whisk in the sugar.

   The mixture will look separated and slightly lumpy.

2. Pour half the butter mixture into the egg and whisk well. Pour the egg and brandy into the rest of the butter mixture. Whisk over very low heat until the sauce is creamy and smooth, about 10 seconds.

   Be careful, high heat will cause the egg to scramble.

MAKES ½ CUP

Poached Pear in Red Wine

THIS IS A DELICIOUS, YET LOW-CALORIE, NONFAT DESSERT. THE WINE-STEEPED PEARS ARE COLORED A VIVID BURGUNDY AND ARE AS PLEASING TO THE EYE AS TO THE PALATE. THE CINNAMON STICK, ALLSPICE, AND LEMON ADD WONDERFUL FLAVOR.

KITCHENWARE: paring knife, juicer, large saucepan, cake tester, tongs

PREPARATION TIME: 25 minutes

COOKING TIME: 30 minutes or more, depending on the ripeness of the pears

POACHING TIME: 15 to 30 minutes

DO-AHEAD: Make the pears a day in advance. Refrigerate, well covered, in the poaching liquid. This will keep the pears moist. If made ahead, serve the pears at room temperature.

1 QUART RED TABLE WINE	10 WHOLE ALLSPICE
1 QUART WATER	JUICE OF 3 LEMONS
3 CUPS SUGAR	8 PEARS (ANJOU OR BARTLETT), PEELED
4 CINNAMON STICKS	

1. Bring the wine, water, sugar, cinnamon, allspice, and lemon juice to a boil in the saucepan. Simmer for 15 minutes. Add the pears and simmer uncovered for 15 minutes. The pears are ready when a tester easily pierces the flesh.

2. Remove from the heat and allow the pears to steep in the poaching liquid for 15 to 30 minutes.

8 SERVINGS

SERVICE: Serve the pears warm or at room temperature, with Raspberry Sauce (page 169), ice cream, or Orange Chantilly Cream (page 163).

COOK'S TIPS:

❖ The raw pears should be firm to the touch, not eating ripe.

❖ The correct "doneness" of the pears is critical. They shouldn't be too hard or too soft.

Raspberry Sauce

RASPBERRY SAUCE IS A GLORIOUS DESSERT GARNISH. ICE CREAM, POUND CAKE, POACHED AND FRESH FRUITS, WARM PIES, AND PUDDINGS ARE ENHANCED BY JUST A FEW SPOONFULS OF OUR BRANDY-SCENTED RASPBERRY SAUCE. WE ALWAYS KEEP A SUPPLY IN THE REFRIGERATOR OR FREEZER.

THE DILEMMA IS TO STRAIN OR NOT TO STRAIN THE RASPBERRIES. THIS DEPENDS ON INDIVIDUAL TASTE. IN THE FIRST METHOD, THE SAUCE IS SILKY AND SMOOTH. IN THE SECOND, THE TEXTURE OF THE SEEDS IS QUITE EVIDENT. WE HAVE CHOSEN TO PUREE AND STRAIN THE RASPBERRIES IN THIS RECIPE.

KITCHENWARE: food processor, small bowl, fine-mesh strainer or sifter, rubber spatula

PREPARATION TIME: 10 minutes

DO-AHEAD: Make the puree and refrigerate in a tightly covered plastic container for up to 3 days. Adjust flavors before using.

1 PINT FRESH RASPBERRIES, OR ONE 12-OUNCE BAG FROZEN, UNSWEETENED, RASPBERRIES, DEFROSTED

3 TABLESPOONS CONFECTIONERS' OR SUPERFINE SUGAR (SEE COOK'S TIP)

1 TEASPOON LEMON JUICE

1/4 TEASPOON PURE VANILLA EXTRACT

1 TEASPOON FRAMBOISE (RASPBERRY BRANDY) OR BRANDY

1. Puree the raspberries in the bowl of the food processor.

2. In a small bowl, combine the puree with the sugar, lemon juice, vanilla, and brandy. Strain the puree.

8 SERVINGS

COOK'S TIP: Granulated sugar will not dissolve and will make this sauce gritty. Use only confectioners' or superfine sugar.

Almond Pudding, Bananas, and Berries

ALMOND PUDDING IS THE SUCCESSFUL RESULT OF MISREADING A RECIPE. WHILE MAKING

CRÈME BRÛLÉE, WE OMITTED ONE CRITICAL STEP: BAKING THE CUSTARD. THE NEW

DESSERT HAD A SMOOTH, THICK CONSISTENCY, NOT THE SILKY, FIRM TEXTURE OF

CRÈME BRÛLÉE. SINCE WASTING FOOD IS OUT OF THE QUESTION, WE

OPTED TO FILE THIS RECIPE UNDER PUDDINGS.

THE RESULT—A DELICIOUS MISTAKE.

KITCHENWARE: chef's knife, medium stainless-steel saucepan, electric mixer with whisk attachment, metal spoon, 3-quart covered serving dish

PREPARATION TIME: 20 minutes

REFRIGERATION TIME: 4 hours

COOKING TIME: 10 minutes

DO-AHEAD: Make the custard a day ahead. Add the fruits and garnish just before serving.

3$\frac{1}{2}$ CUPS HEAVY CREAM OR MILK

4 EGG YOLKS PLUS 4 LARGE EGGS

$\frac{1}{2}$ CUP SUGAR

2 TEASPOONS PURE VANILLA EXTRACT

2 TEASPOONS ALMOND EXTRACT

2 BANANAS, THINLY SLICED

1 PINT STRAWBERRIES, WASHED, HULLED, AND THINLY SLICED

GARNISH:

WHOLE STRAWBERRIES

1. Scald the cream or milk in the saucepan and remove from the heat.

   To "scald," bring to a boil and immediately remove from the heat.

2. Beat the egg yolks, eggs, and sugar in the bowl of the electric mixer until thick and lemon colored, 3 to 4 minutes. Blend in the vanilla and almond extracts.

3. On medium speed, pour the cream in a slow, steady stream into the egg mixture and mix well.

4. Pour the entire mixture back into the saucepan. Simmer over low heat for 5 minutes, stirring constantly, until the custard is thick enough to coat a metal spoon.

5. Pour the custard into the serving dish. Cool to room temperature, cover, and refrigerate for 4 hours or overnight.

10 SERVINGS

SERVICE: Just before serving, gently fold the sliced bananas and strawberries into the custard. Spoon the custard into red wine glasses, compote coupes, or individual dessert bowls. Top each dish with whole berries.

If you combine the fruit and custard ahead, the natural juices of the fruit will make the custard watery.

COOK'S TIP: Infuse the heady flavor of eggnog into the custard by substituting rum for the almond extract.

Tappan Hill Brownies

THESE BROWNIES ARE REMINISCENT OF THE MANY CHOCOLATE WEDDING CAKES SERVED AT TAPPAN HILL. OUR BRIDES AND GROOMS CLAMOR FOR THE RECIPE WHEN CELEBRATING THEIR FIRST ANNIVERSARY.

KITCHENWARE: chopper, medium-size heavy-bottomed saucepan, small bowl, rubber spatula, electric mixer with whisk attachment, 8 × 11 × 2-inch cake pan, cake tester

PREPARATION TIME: 25 minutes

COOKING TIME: 2 minutes

BAKING TIME: 40 minutes

DO-AHEAD: Make the brownies 2 weeks ahead. Freeze, well covered. (Our favorite treat is munching on *frozen* Tappan Hill Brownies.)

---

8 OUNCES SEMISWEET BAKING CHOCOLATE (BAKER'S OR GHIRADELLI)

2 OUNCES UNSWEETENED CHOCOLATE

8 OUNCES (2 STICKS) SWEET BUTTER

1/2 CUP FLOUR

1 1/2 TEASPOONS BAKING POWDER

1/2 TEASPOON SALT

3 EGGS

1 CUP PLUS 2 TABLESPOONS SUGAR

1 TABLESPOON PURE VANILLA EXTRACT

1 1/2 CUPS SEMISWEET CHOCOLATE MORSELS

1 1/2 CUPS CHOPPED WALNUTS

---

1. Preheat the oven to 350 degrees. Grease the baking pan and dust lightly with flour.

2. Break the semisweet and unsweetened chocolate into 1-ounce pieces. Bring the butter to a boil in a heavy-bottomed saucepan. Add both chocolates and immediately remove from the heat. Stir until the chocolate melts completely.

   Here, we prefer solid chocolate to the morsels. The consistency of melted morsels tends to be gooey instead of smooth.

3. Combine the flour, baking powder, and salt in a small bowl and set aside.

4. Combine the eggs and sugar in the bowl of the electric mixer. Beat until the mixture is very thick and forms ribbons when you lift the beaters away from the batter. Add the vanilla and blend lightly. Add the melted chocolate and mix lightly.

5. Gently fold the flour mixture into the chocolate batter with a spatula. Fold in the chocolate morsels and nuts.

6. Spread the batter in the greased baking pan. Bake for 35 to 40 minutes. When done, a cake tester inserted into the center of the brownies will have a little batter clinging to it.

   Do not overbake the brownies. They are super-delicious when a little wet and "gooey."

7. Cool the brownies in the baking pan.

20 BROWNIES

SERVICE: Cut the brownies into $1\frac{1}{2}$-inch squares. Serve with fresh fruit, or topped with ice cream for a sinfully rich brownie sundae.

COOK'S TIPS:

❖ The brownies will become crumbly and dry if overbaked.

❖ Nuts can be omitted from the recipe. (We've discovered that most young children don't like nuts.)

Chapter 9

Menus

A CORNUCOPIA OF BRUNCH

TAILGATE ANTICS

THE ROAST CHICKEN DINNER

AN INFORMAL BARBECUE

A HOWLING HALLOWEEN

FONDUE FRENZY

THE DINNER PARTY

IN THIS SECTION, WE'VE PUT RECIPES TOGETHER TO CREATE SPECIAL-OCCASION MENUS.
EACH MENU INCLUDES "COOKING TOGETHER," OUR TIMETABLE SUGGESTING HOW
CHORES CAN BE DIVIDED. TWO COOKS CAN WORK MORE QUICKLY
AND EFFICIENTLY THAN ONE.

IN TIME, AS YOU GAIN EXPERIENCE, YOU MAY FIND THAT A DIFFERENT DIVISION OF CHORES
WORKS BETTER FOR YOU. THAT'S FINE. THESE ARE SIMPLY SUGGESTED TIMETABLES.
ONE OF YOU MAY HAVE MORE TIME AVAILABLE ON ANY GIVEN DAY. ONE MAY
PREFER SLICING AND DICING, WHILE THE OTHER PREFERS TO DO THE
ACTUAL COOKING. THE ULTIMATE DECISION ON WHO DOES WHAT AND
WHEN DEPENDS ON WHAT WORKS BEST FOR YOU.

DON'T HESITATE TO SUBSTITUTE RECIPES FROM THE FRONT SECTION FOR
THOSE IN THESE MENUS.

A Cornucopia of Brunch

(ALL RECIPES SERVE 4)

MENU

DOUBLE-DIPPED CHALLAH FRENCH TOAST WITH WARM POACHED ORANGE SYRUP

JALAPEÑO PEPPER MONTEREY JACK FRITTATA

CUCUMBER, RADISH, AND SOUR CREAM SALAD

MOSAICS OF FRUIT WITH COCONUT

CURRANT-GINGER CRISPS

SUGGESTED WINE: Van Der Kamp "Midnight Cuvee" Rosé Sparkling Wine, Sonoma County, California

Brunch includes some of the most enjoyable foods we eat. Menu ideas are endless. The setting can be casual or formal, with every season the right season for a buffet of favorite foods. A colorful table laden with fresh fruits, varieties of hearty breads, butters infused with preserves, and at least two different flavored coffees sets the scene for a warm and friendly party.

Plain white china and floral napkins, or flowery china and napkins in solid colors complete the picture.

Double-Dipped Challah French Toast with Warm Poached Orange Syrup

THICK, GOLDEN, FLUFFY SLICES OF CHALLAH FRENCH TOAST DRIPPING WITH REAL HONEST-TO-GOODNESS MAPLE SYRUP IS OUR FAVORITE BRUNCH DISH. SINCE THE BREAD SOAKS UP THE EGGS AND CREAM, YOU ARE REWARDED WITH LIGHT AIRY TOAST. CERTAINLY THE TOAST CAN STAND ALONE; HOWEVER, SURROUND IT WITH STRIPS OF BACON, CRISPY SAUSAGE, OR SLICES OF HAM FOR AN ADDED TREAT.

KITCHENWARE: chef's knife, serrated knife, large mixing bowl, whisk, large sauté pan, baking pan, aluminum foil, fine-mesh strainer or sifter

PREPARATION TIME: 10 minutes (not including Poached Orange Syrup)

COOKING TIME: 12 minutes

6 EGGS

3/4 CUP HEAVY CREAM OR MILK

1 TEASPOON PURE VANILLA EXTRACT

1/4 CUP HONEY

1 TABLESPOON GRANULATED SUGAR

1/2 TEASPOON GROUND CINNAMON

2 TABLESPOONS MINCED ORANGE ZEST

1 POUND SQUARE CHALLAH BREAD, CUT INTO EIGHT 1 1/2-INCH SLICES

8 TABLESPOONS (1 STICK) SWEET BUTTER

1 RECIPE WARM POACHED ORANGE SYRUP (RECIPE FOLLOWS)

GARNISH:

CONFECTIONERS' SUGAR

Use regular challah loaves if square ones are unavailable.

1. Preheat the oven to 200 degrees.

2. Whisk the eggs in a large bowl until mixed. Add the cream or milk, vanilla, honey, granulated sugar, cinnamon, and orange zest. Blend all the ingredients with the whisk.

Continued

3. Dip both sides of the challah slices twice into the cream mixture.

4. Heat the butter in the sauté pan until hot.

   Do not brown the butter or the toast will have a burnt taste. Between batches wipe the pan clean. This will keep the butter fresh and the toast golden.

   Sauté the first batch of slices for 2 to 3 minutes on each side, until golden. Transfer the bread to the baking pan and cover with foil. Make the remaining toast. The toast can stay in the oven for 20 minutes without drying out.

5. Make the orange syrup.

SERVICE: Sift a light coating of confectioners' sugar over the toast. Serve with Warm Poached Orange Syrup on the side.

COOK'S TIPS:

❖ Thick slices of French bread or brioche make fine French toast.

❖ Warm Poached Orange Syrup makes a great topping for ice cream, sponge cake, and custards.

WARM POACHED ORANGE SYRUP

KITCHENWARE: utility knife, small saucepan, small strainer

PREPARATION TIME: 10 minutes

COOKING TIME: 4 minutes

2 CUPS PURE MAPLE SYRUP	ZEST OF 1 SMALL LEMON
4 LARGE EATING ORANGES, PEELED AND SECTIONED	½ CUP GOLDEN RAISINS

1. Gently warm the syrup in the saucepan over low heat. Do not boil.

2. Add the orange sections, lemon zest, and raisins to the maple syrup. Simmer for 3 minutes.

MAKES 2 TO 3 CUPS

Jalapeño Pepper Monterey Jack Frittata

HERE'S AN EASY WAY TO SERVE EGGS WITHOUT THE ANXIETY OF LAST-MINUTE COOKING. THE FRITTATA CAN BE SERVED WARM OR COLD. ITS SPICY TASTE COMPLEMENTS THE MELLOW CHALLAH FRENCH TOAST.

KITCHENWARE: chef's knife, grater, pepper mill, large ovenproof skillet, whisk, spatula

PREPARATION TIME: 20 minutes

COOKING TIME: 25 minutes

4 TABLESPOONS VIRGIN OLIVE OIL

1 RED BELL PEPPER, SEEDED AND DICED

2 SCALLIONS (WHITE PART ONLY), THINLY SLICED

1 LARGE TOMATO, DICED

2 TEASPOONS CHOPPED FRESH CILANTRO

8 EGGS, BEATEN

¾ CUP GRATED JALAPEÑO MONTEREY JACK CHEESE

¾ CUP GRATED MONTEREY JACK CHEESE

¼ POUND COUNTRY SMOKED HAM, JULIENNED

SALT AND FRESHLY GROUND PEPPER

1. Preheat the oven to 350 degrees.

2. Heat the oil in the skillet. Sauté the pepper and scallions for 3 to 4 minutes, until soft. Add the tomato and cilantro and sauté for 1 minute. Whisk the eggs, cheeses, ham, salt, and pepper into the pan.

3. Cook the frittata over low heat for 2 to 3 minutes. As the eggs begin to set, lift and tilt the uncooked portion over the set edges.

4. Put the frittata in the oven for 12 to 15 minutes, until the eggs have set.

Continued

SERVICE: Serve the frittata right in the skillet. Let your guests help themselves.

COOK'S TIPS:

❖ The adaptable frittata can be served hot or cold.

❖ Sandwich the frittata between slices of buttered French bread and take it along on a picnic or cut it up into small wedges as an hors d'oeuvre.

❖ Add leftover veggies or cooked meats to the eggs and serve for lunch or a light supper.

Cucumber, Radish, and Sour Cream Salad

WE LOVE THE TINGLING SENSATION OF THE RADISH COMBINED WITH THE SMOOTHNESS OF THE SOUR CREAM AND FONDLY CALL THIS DISH "VEGETABLE CHOP SUEY."

KITCHENWARE: chef's knife, pepper mill, medium mixing bowl

PREPARATION TIME: 15 minutes

MARINATING TIME: 20 minutes

1 SMALL CLOVE GARLIC, MINCED

1 TEASPOON TARRAGON VINEGAR

1/2 CUP SOUR CREAM

1/2 TEASPOON GROUND GREEN PEPPERCORNS

1 LARGE CUCUMBER, CUT INTO 1/4-INCH-THICK SLICES

12 LARGE RADISHES, THINLY SLICED

SALT

GARNISH:

1/2 TEASPOON CHOPPED FRESH TARRAGON

1. Combine the garlic, vinegar, sour cream, and green peppercorns in the mixing bowl. Let stand for 5 minutes.

2. Blend the cucumber and radishes with the sour cream mixture and season with salt. Marinate in the refrigerator for 20 minutes before serving.

   If you add the sour cream to the vegetables more than 20 minutes before serving, the natural juices from the cucumber will thin the sour cream into a runny sauce.

SERVICE: Fill a glass serving bowl with the Cucumber, Radish, and Sour Cream Salad. Garnish the top with the chopped tarragon.

COOK'S TIPS:

❖ Yogurt can be used in place of the sour cream; the sauce will have a thinner consistency.

❖ The cucumber/radish combination creates a refreshing accent for fish or chicken.

Mosaics of Fruit with Coconut

WE ENJOY THE COOL, REFRESHING TASTE OF FRUIT DURING AND AFTER BRUNCH.
RIPE PEACHES, APRICOTS, AND PLUMS ARE GOOD OPTIONS FOR THE FRUIT MIX.

KITCHENWARE: baking sheet, medium mixing bowl, small knife

PREPARATION TIME: 20 minutes

COOKING TIME: 8 minutes

MARINATING TIME: 2 hours

$\frac{1}{2}$ CUP CANNED OR BAGGED SWEETENED COCONUT

$\frac{1}{2}$ CUP ORANGE JUICE

$\frac{1}{3}$ CUP DRY WHITE WINE

$\frac{1}{4}$ CUP KIRSCH LIQUEUR OR BRANDY

1 PINT STRAWBERRIES

2 MANGOES

2 KIWIS

1. Preheat the oven to 350 degrees.

2. Spread the coconut on the baking sheet and toast in the oven for 8 minutes, until golden.

3. Blend the orange juice, wine, and liqueur in the mixing bowl.

4. Stem and hull the strawberries and cut them in half. Peel the mangoes and quarter the fruit around the pits. Cut each quarter in half. Peel and cut the kiwis into $\frac{1}{4}$-inch slices.

5. Marinate the fruit in the juice mixture for 2 hours.

    Do not marinate the fruit longer than 2 hours. The acid from the orange juice will cause the fruit to fall apart.

SERVICE: Serve the fruit topped with the coconut in individual dishes or in one serving bowl.

COOK'S TIP: Fresh fruit recipes can easily be doubled without losing their flavor.

Currant-Ginger Crisps

THE CRYSTALLIZED GINGER IN THESE CRISPS CREATES AN UNEXPECTED TINGLING SENSATION WHEN YOU BITE INTO THEM.

KITCHENWARE: chef's knife, small cup, electric mixer with whisk attachment, rubber spatula, plastic wrap, baking sheet, metal spatula, cooling rack

PREPARATION TIME: 15 minutes

CHILLING TIME: 1 hour

BAKING TIME: 10 minutes

3 TABLESPOONS CURRANTS	**1 TABLESPOON PURE VANILLA EXTRACT**
¹/₄ CUP BRANDY	**¹/₂ CUP CHOPPED CRYSTALLIZED GINGER**
12 TABLESPOONS (1 ¹/₂ STICKS) SWEET BUTTER	**³/₄ CUP FLOUR**
3 TABLESPOONS CONFECTIONERS' SUGAR	

1. Soak and plump the currants in the brandy in the small cup for 10 minutes.

2. Place the butter and sugar in the bowl of the electric mixer and beat until creamy. Scrape down the sides of the bowl.

3. Add the vanilla, ginger, drained currants, and flour. Beat the mixture until the ingredients are well blended.

4. Form the dough into a 1¹/₂-inch-wide roll. Seal the roll in plastic wrap. Chill well, about 1 hour.

   Chilling the dough is crucial for easy handling.

5. Twenty minutes before baking, preheat the oven to 350 degrees. Cut the cookies into ¹/₈-inch slices. Arrange on the baking sheet 1¹/₂ inches apart and bake for 7 to 10 minutes, until lightly brown and crisp. With the metal spatula, place the cookies on the cooling rack.

Continued

SERVICE: Serve the cookies with fruit, ice cream, or sorbet. Dip the crisps in warm chocolate sauce for a special treat.

COOK'S TIPS:

❖   Double the recipe and keep the unbaked cookies in the freezer. Defrost the unbaked cookie dough in the refrigerator.

❖   Baked cookies can be stored at room temperature or in the freezer in an airtight container.

Cooking Together
A Cornucopia of Brunch

SEVERAL DAYS IN ADVANCE

COOK 1: CURRANT-GINGER CRISPS

Bake and freeze.

THE NIGHT BEFORE

COOK 1: DOUBLE-DIPPED CHALLAH FRENCH TOAST

Slice the challah. Cover well with plastic wrap and store at room temperature. Combine all the ingredients in step 2, cover, and refrigerate.

CUCUMBER, RADISH, AND SOUR CREAM SALAD

Slice the cucumbers and radishes. Seal well with plastic wrap and store in the refrigerator. Chop the tarragon. Seal and refrigerate.

MOSAICS OF FRUIT WITH COCONUT

Toast the coconut. Cover well and store at room temperature. Blend the juice, wine, and liqueur. Store at room temperature.

COOK 2: JALAPEÑO PEPPER MONTEREY JACK FRITTATA

Prepare the pepper, scallions, tomato, and cilantro. Grate the cheeses, julienne the ham, and break the eggs. Refrigerate all the ingredients separately, tightly covered.

WARM POACHED ORANGE SYRUP

Peel and section the oranges. Refrigerate, well covered.

The Morning of the Brunch

Cook 1: **Currant-Ginger Crisps**

Defrost and arrange the cookies.

Double-Dipped Challah French Toast

Dip the challah.

Cook 2: **Warm Poached Orange Syrup**

Make the Warm Poached Orange Syrup.

Mosaics of Fruit with Coconut

Prepare and marinate the fruit.

Together: Prepare all garnishes.

One Hour Before Brunch

Cook 1: **Double-Dipped Challah French Toast**

Preheat the oven. Sauté the challah and keep warm in the oven.

Cucumber, Radish, and Sour Cream Salad

Prepare the marinade and marinate the cucumbers and radishes 20 minutes before serving.

Cook 2: **Jalapeño Pepper Monterey Jack Frittata**

Make the frittata and keep warm in the oven.

Mosaics of Fruit with Coconut

Transfer the fruit to a serving bowl.

Together: Arrange and garnish the brunch.

Tailgate Antics

(ALL RECIPES SERVE 4)

MENU

BEER-SPIKED CHEDDAR CHEESE SOUP

SAUSAGE AND EGGPLANT PITA POCKETS

TORTELLINI SALAD WITH SMOKED GOUDA CHEESE

BRANDIED APPLE-PEAR CAKE

SUGGESTED WINES: Hidden Cellars Sauvignon Blanc, Mendocino County, California

Millbrook Cabernet Franc, Hudson Valley, New York

Ravenswood Zinfandel Vintners Blend, Sonoma County, California

COOKING THE FOOD ISN'T THE REAL CHALLENGE! FINDING ENOUGH SPACE IN OUR 4 x 4

FOR FAMILY AND FRIENDS, THE DELECTABLE FOODS WE'VE PREPARED, THE COOLER,

SIX PACKS OF BEER, SOFT DRINKS, MIXERS, WARM LINED GLOVES, HATS,

SCARVES, AND BLANKETS IS THE REAL TEST!

IT IS A GOOD IDEA TO BUY THE BEST-QUALITY PAPER PLATES AND PLASTIC UTENSILS;

THERE IS NOTHING MORE ANNOYING THAN WATCHING YOUR LUNCH FALL THROUGH THE

BOTTOM OF A SOGGY, THIN PAPER PLATE. COLOR-COORDINATE THE UTENSILS, DISHES, AND

NAPKINS AND BRING EXTRAS OF EVERYTHING FOR UNFORESEEN HAPPENINGS.

DON'T FORGET THE GARBAGE BAGS FOR QUICK CLEANUP!

FOOTBALL GAMES ARE MORE ENJOYABLE WHEN VIEWED ON A FULL STOMACH, AND

APPETITES SEEM TO EXPAND AS THE TEMPERATURE DIPS. (WE ALWAYS INCLUDE A HOT

THERMOS OF COFFEE AND/OR COCOA FOR ALL OUTDOOR EVENTS.)

Beer-Spiked Cheddar Cheese Soup

FROSTY WEEKEND AFTERNOONS, STEAMING CHEDDAR CHEESE SOUP, AND WINNING FOOTBALL
ARE THE MAGICAL INGREDIENTS FOR SUCCESSFUL TAILGATING. TO FIGHT OFF THE AUTUMN
CHILL, WE "OVERDASH" THE CAYENNE, ADDING A TOUCH OF FIRE TO THE SOUP.

KITCHENWARE: grater, chef's knife, pepper mill, large saucepan, small saucepan, large Thermos

PREPARATION TIME: 25 minutes

COOKING TIME: 10 minutes

3 TABLESPOONS SWEET BUTTER

1 MEDIUM ONION, FINELY CHOPPED

1 MEDIUM CARROT, PEELED AND FINELY
CHOPPED

1 STALK CELERY, FINELY CHOPPED

3 TABLESPOONS FLOUR

1 CUP CHICKEN BROTH (FRESH OR
CANNED, UNSALTED)

2 CUPS MILK

2 CUPS GRATED EXTRA-SHARP CHEDDAR
CHEESE

1/2 CUP BEER, AT ROOM TEMPERATURE

DASH OF CAYENNE

1/8 TEASPOON SALT

1/8 TEASPOON FRESHLY GROUND BLACK
PEPPER

3 TABLESPOONS CHOPPED FRESH CHIVES

1. Melt the butter in the large heavy saucepan. Add the onion, carrot, and celery and sauté until the vegetables are lightly golden, about 3 minutes. Add the flour and blend well with the vegetables.

2. Warm the chicken broth and milk in the smaller saucepan and slowly add this mixture to the vegetables. Simmer over moderate heat, stirring until the soup thickens, about 4 minutes.

3. Blend in the cheese and beer, stirring until the cheese has melted. Season with cayenne, salt, and pepper. Blend the chives into the soup.

SERVICE: Pour very hot water into the soup Thermos and let it stand for about 10 minutes to heat the inside lining. Drain the Thermos well before filling it with Beer-Spiked Cheddar Cheese Soup.

COOK'S TIP: To serve at home, fill crocks and garnish each crock with chives instead of blending the chives into the soup in step 3.

Sausage and Eggplant Pita Pockets

THIS SANDWICH IS A MEAL IN ITSELF. YOU CAN REALLY TASTE THE INDIVIDUAL CHARACTER OF THE VEGETABLES, SWEET SAUSAGE, AND SHARP CHEESE WITH EACH BITE. HOW WONDERFUL TO BE ABLE TO SATISFY A ROBUST APPETITE SO EASILY.

KITCHENWARE: chef's knife, grater, pepper mill, large sauté pan, tongs

PREPARATION TIME: 25 minutes

COOKING TIME: 20 minutes

1 TABLESPOON VIRGIN OLIVE OIL	1 TEASPOON DRIED OREGANO
1 POUND ITALIAN SWEET SAUSAGE, CUT INTO 1-INCH PIECES	1 CLOVE GARLIC, MINCED
1 MEDIUM RED ONION, DICED	1 CUP RED WINE
2 RED BELL PEPPERS, SEEDED AND JULIENNED	1/2 CUP GRATED SHARP PECORINO CHEESE
1 SMALL EGGPLANT, DICED	SALT AND FRESHLY GROUND PEPPER
	4 LARGE PITA POCKETS

1. Heat the oil in the sauté pan. Brown the sausage pieces on all sides. Add the onion, red bell peppers, eggplant, and oregano. Cook until the vegetables are almost soft, about 5 minutes.

2. Add the garlic and cook for 30 seconds. Add the wine and cook for 4 minutes more. Blend in the cheese and season with salt and pepper.

   The filling does not have to be hot to be delicious; relax and fill the pockets ahead of time. However, if you have more than an hour's drive, fill the pockets just before eating. The bread tends to become soggy when the filling sits too long.

SERVICE: Heap the pita pockets with the filling and fold the top over to seal. Wrap each pita in aluminum foil.

COOK'S TIPS:

- ❖ Pack lots of big napkins and wet wipes; this is a drippy sandwich.

- ❖ Put the filling into a large-mouth Thermos. Let your fellow tailgaters stuff their own pita pockets.

Tortellini Salad with Smoked Gouda Cheese

"Stick-to-your-ribs" foods are essential for tailgating. Sitting in a stadium on a frosty afternoon in November, after the sun's last rays have disappeared, calls for thick sweaters and a well-fueled body. This tangy recipe fills the bill.

KITCHENWARE: chef's knife, pepper mill, large saucepan, colander, medium saucepan, large mixing bowl, whisk

PREPARATION TIME: 30 minutes

COOKING TIME: 15 minutes

6 QUARTS WATER

1 TABLESPOON SALT

1 POUND FROZEN CHEESE TORTELLINI

1 LARGE CARROT, PEELED AND JULIENNED INTO 2-INCH STRIPS

1 CUP BROCCOLI FLORETS

1 SMALL ZUCCHINI, HALVED AND JULIENNED INTO 2-INCH STRIPS

2 CLOVES GARLIC, MINCED

1/2 CUP VIRGIN OLIVE OIL

1/4 CUP BALSAMIC VINEGAR

1 TABLESPOON CHOPPED FRESH BASIL

1 TABLESPOON CHOPPED FRESH FLAT-LEAF PARSLEY

12 MEDIUM CHERRY TOMATOES, HALVED

1/2 CUP PITTED GREEN OLIVE HALVES

4 OUNCES SMOKED GOUDA, CUT INTO 1/2-INCH CUBES

SALT AND FRESHLY GROUND PEPPER

1. In the large saucepan, bring 4 quarts of the water to a boil. Add the tablespoon of salt. Place the tortellini in the water and stir gently. Simmer the pasta, uncovered, for 9 minutes. Drain the pasta through the colander and rinse with cold water.

Continued

2. Bring the remaining 2 quarts of water to a boil in the medium saucepan. Blanch the carrot for 1 minute. Add the broccoli and zucchini and cook for 30 seconds. Drain the vegetables. Run cold water through the vegetables to stop the cooking process and keep them crisp.

3. Whisk the garlic, oil, vinegar, basil, and parsley in a large bowl. Toss the vinaigrette with the tomatoes, olives, tortellini, blanched vegetables, and cheese. Season with salt and pepper.

SERVICE: Pile the pasta into a large plastic container fitted with a tight lid or into 4 individual serving containers with lids.

COOK'S TIP: Turn Tortellini Salad into a main dish by adding chunks of Italian cured salami or smoked ham. Crusty bread and chilled fresh fruit complete the menu.

Brandied Apple-Pear Cake

THIS VERSATILE CAKE ADAPTS WELL FOR TAILGATING, BRUNCHES, SNACKING, AND TEA. IF YOU
KEEP IT TIGHTLY WRAPPED, THE FRESHNESS WILL LINGER AND YOU WILL BE ABLE TO
TASTE THE MELLOWNESS OF THE FRUIT, SPICES, VANILLA, AND BRANDY.

KITCHENWARE: chef's knife, paring knife, electric mixer with whisk attachment, rubber spatula, nonstick $9^{1}/_{4} \times 5^{1}/_{4} \times 2^{3}/_{4}$-inch loaf pan (or loaf pan and nonstick cooking spray), cake tester, cooling rack

PREPARATION TIME: 25 minutes

BAKING TIME: 1 hour 20 minutes

1 1/2 CUPS FLOUR	1 TABLESPOON PURE VANILLA EXTRACT
1 1/2 TEASPOONS BAKING POWDER	2/3 CUP SUGAR
1/2 TEASPOON SALT	1 GRANNY SMITH APPLE, PEELED, CORED, AND DICED
2 TEASPOONS GROUND CINNAMON	
2 EGGS, BEATEN	1 RIPE PEAR, PEELED, CORED, AND DICED
1 CUP OIL (CANOLA, CORN, OR SUNFLOWER)	1/4 CUP RAISINS
1/3 CUP ORANGE JUICE	1 TABLESPOON WALNUT OR PECAN PIECES
1 1/2 TABLESPOONS CALVADOS OR APPLEJACK BRANDY	

1. Preheat the oven to 350 degrees.

2. Combine the flour, baking powder, salt, and cinnamon in the bowl of the electric mixer. Mix well.

3. With the beater on low, slowly add the eggs, oil, orange juice, brandy, vanilla, and sugar. Beat on medium until all the ingredients are just incorporated.

Continued

4. Add the apple, pear, raisins, and nuts and blend on low. Pour the batter into the nonstick loaf pan. Bake for 1 hour and 20 minutes, or until a cake tester inserted in the center comes out clean. Cool the cake on the rack.

The lengthy baking time is due to the abundant moisture of the fruit juices in the cake.

SERVICE: Cut the cooled cake into serving pieces. Tightly wrap each piece in foil before packing to preserve its freshness.

COOK'S TIP: Brandied Apple-Pear Cake freezes very well.

Cooking Together
Tailgate Antics

SEVERAL DAYS IN ADVANCE

COOK 1: SAUSAGE AND EGGPLANT PITA POCKETS

BEER-SPIKED CHEDDAR CHEESE SOUP

Dice the onion and seed and julienne the red bell peppers for the pita pockets. Wrap well and refrigerate. Chop the onion, carrot, and celery for the soup. Wrap well and refrigerate. Grate the Cheddar cheese for the soup and the Pecorino cheese for the pita pockets. Seal separately in plastic wrap and refrigerate.

COOK 2: BRANDIED APPLE-PEAR CAKE

Bake the cake, cool, wrap well, and store in the freezer.

TORTELLINI SALAD WITH SMOKED GOUDA CHEESE

While the cake is baking, prepare the carrot for the tortellini, halve the olives, and cube the Gouda. Refrigerate individually, well covered. Help with the chopping and grating.

WHOEVER HAS TIME: Make the vinaigrette for the tortellini.

THE NIGHT BEFORE

COOK 1: BEER-SPIKED CHEDDAR CHEESE SOUP

Make the soup, cool, and refrigerate, covered. Do not add the chives. Find the soup Thermos.

BRANDIED APPLE-PEAR CAKE

Transfer the cake from the freezer to the refrigerator.

COOK 2: **SAUSAGE AND EGGPLANT PITA POCKETS**

Cut up and brown the sausage. Cool and refrigerate, covered.

TORTELLINI SALAD WITH SMOKED GOUDA CHEESE

Cook the tortellini, prepare the broccoli, blanch and cool the vegetables. Toss the tortellini with the vinaigrette, cover, and refrigerate. Cover and refrigerate the vegetables separately.

TOGETHER: Prepare all the garnishes.

THE MORNING OF THE PICNIC

COOK 1: **BEER-SPIKED CHEDDAR CHEESE SOUP**

Fill the Thermos with hot water. Heat the soup. Discard the hot water and fill the Thermos with the soup.

SAUSAGE AND EGGPLANT PITA POCKETS

Complete the pita pocket recipe. Stuff the pockets and wrap in foil.

COOK 2: **TORTELLINI SALAD WITH SMOKED GOUDA CHEESE**

Toss the pasta with the vegetables, reseason to taste. Put into picnic containers.

BRANDIED APPLE-PEAR CAKE

Slice and wrap the cake.

ONE HOUR BEFORE LEAVING FOR THE PICNIC

TOGETHER: Check the kitchen for any food you may have forgotten!

$$

The Roast Chicken Dinner

(ALL RECIPES SERVE 4)

MENU

ORANGE, GRAPEFRUIT, AND AVOCADO SALAD WITH CREAMY AVOCADO DRESSING

ROAST CHICKEN WITH ROOT VEGETABLES

TURKISH RICE PILAF

STRAWBERRY SHORTCAKE CREAM PUFFS

SUGGESTED WINES: Flora Springs Chardonnay "Floral," Napa Valley, California

Mill Creek Merlot, Sonoma County, California

WHEN I WAS GROWING UP, I ALWAYS KNEW WHAT DAY IT WAS BY THE COOKING AROMAS
EMANATING FROM THE KITCHEN! FRIDAY NIGHTS WERE MY FAVORITE BECAUSE WE
LUXURIATED IN MOM'S GOLDEN ROASTED CHICKEN, HER *PIÈCE DE LA RÉSISTANCE*.
THIS MEAL WAS THE HIGHLIGHT OF OUR WEEK; SIMPLE, HEARTY, HEAVENLY
FOOD THAT OUR FAMILY LOOKED FORWARD TO WITH GREAT APPETITE.
EVERY WEEK MOM FOLLOWED HER RIGID DINNER SCHEDULE,
AND EVEN THOUGH WE KNEW WHAT TO EXPECT,
WE WERE NEVER DISAPPOINTED.

ENJOY YOUR ROAST CHICKEN DINNER IN A COZY ENVIRONMENT. SET THE TABLE WITH
EVERYDAY DISHES AND CLAY POTS FILLED WITH AN ASSORTMENT OF
BRIGHTLY COLORED FLOWERS. FOR AN ADDED GLOW,
LIGHT LONG TAPERED CANDLES.

☆Orange, Grapefruit, and Avocado Salad with Creamy Avocado Dressing

SUE AND I ENJOY DEVOURING OUR AVOCADOS HEAPED WITH CHICKEN OR SEAFOOD, OR SIMPLY
SLATHERED WITH RUSSIAN DRESSING. FRUIT SALAD WITH AVOCADO, SAUCED WITH
CREAMY AVOCADO DRESSING, IS OUR IDEA OF PURE JOY.

KITCHENWARE: small paring knife, chef's knife

PREPARATION TIME: 25 minutes (not including Creamy Avocado Dressing)

1 RECIPE CREAMY AVOCADO DRESSING
(RECIPE FOLLOWS)

2 SEEDLESS ORANGES

1 SMALL SEEDLESS GRAPEFRUIT

2 RIPE AVOCADOS

1.   Prepare the dressing and set aside.

2.   Peel the skin from the oranges and grapefruit. Trim off any remaining white pith clinging to the fruit. Cut the fruit into sections.

3.   Cut the avocados in half lengthwise around the pit. Rotate both sides and separate the halves. Cut the unpeeled halves into 4 pieces and remove the peel.

   If you must peel the avocados in advance, put the pieces in a mixture of cold water and lemon juice to prevent discoloration, but don't do this more than 30 minutes before serving.

SERVICE: On a serving platter or individual salad plates, arrange the fruit in overlapping pieces. Alternate the orange and grapefruit sections. Place the avocado slices in the center and drizzle Creamy Avocado Dressing over the fruit.

COOK'S TIP: Creamy Avocado Dressing is delightful tossed with seafood salad.

Continued

CREAMY AVOCADO DRESSING

KITCHENWARE: chef's knife, pepper mill, food processor, spatula, small bowl

PREPARATION TIME: 15 minutes

1 RIPE AVOCADO, PEELED, CUT INTO CHUNKS

1 CUP HEAVY CREAM

JUICE OF 1 LIME

1 TEASPOON WORCESTERSHIRE SAUCE

3 DASHES TABASCO SAUCE

1/8 TEASPOON FRESHLY GROUND PEPPER

1/4 TEASPOON SALT

2 TEASPOONS FINELY CHOPPED FRESH CILANTRO

1 TABLESPOON FINELY CHOPPED RED ONION

1. Put the avocado in the bowl of the food processor. Process until smooth. Add the heavy cream, lime juice, Worcestershire sauce, Tabasco, pepper, salt, and cilantro. Pulse twice to blend.

2. Put the dressing in a small bowl and fold in the onion.

MAKES 1 1/2 CUPS

Roast Chicken with Root Vegetables

THE SECRET TO MOM'S ROAST CHICKEN WAS TWO HUGE, ROUGHLY CHOPPED SPANISH ONIONS ADDED TO THE ROASTING PAN BEFORE PUTTING THE CHICKEN INTO THE OVEN. THE CAPTIVATING AROMA OF THE ONIONS CARAMELIZING IN THE NATURAL DRIPPINGS FROM THE CHICKEN MADE ME BRAZEN ENOUGH TO PINCH A LITTLE PIECE OF CHICKEN WHEN NO ONE WAS LOOKING.

KITCHENWARE: chef's knife, pepper mill, vegetable peeler, grater, small mixing bowl, wooden spoon, roasting pan

PREPARATION TIME: 30 minutes

ROASTING TIME: 45 minutes

8 TABLESPOONS (1 STICK) SWEET BUTTER, SOFTENED

1 TEASPOON DIJON MUSTARD

2 CLOVES GARLIC, MINCED

1 TABLESPOON LEMON JUICE

GRATED ZEST OF 1 LEMON

$^1/_2$ TEASPOON CHOPPED FRESH ROSEMARY

$^1/_8$ TEASPOON SALT

$^1/_4$ TEASPOON FRESHLY GROUND PEPPER

2 BROILER CHICKENS, 3–3$^1/_2$ POUNDS EACH, CUT INTO QUARTERS

2 LARGE SPANISH ONIONS, THINLY SLICED

3 SMALL CARROTS, PEELED AND CUT INTO $^1/_2$-INCH DICE

1 LARGE TURNIP, PEELED AND CUT INTO $^1/_2$-INCH DICE

1. Preheat the oven to 400 degrees.

2. Using the wooden spoon, combine the butter, mustard, half the garlic, the lemon juice, zest, rosemary, salt, and pepper in the mixing bowl until well blended.

3. Loosen the chicken skin by lifting it gently from the flesh with your fingers. The skin will lift quite easily.

Continued

Make sure the edges of the skin remain attached to the flesh.

4. Reserving 2 tablespoons, spread the herbed butter under the skin. Lightly spread the remaining butter over the chicken pieces.

5. Put the onions, carrots, turnip, and the rest of the garlic into the roasting pan. Place the chicken on the bed of vegetables. Roast for 40 to 45 minutes, until the chicken is golden brown and cooked through.

SERVICE: Serve 2 pieces of chicken with roasted vegetables per person.

COOK'S TIP: Roast these vegetables in the herbed butter and serve as a side dish with any main course.

Turkish Rice Pilaf

THE COLORS AND FLAVORS OF THE PILAF REMIND US OF THE ROMANCE AND MAGIC OF THE
EASTERN MEDITERRANEAN. THE MARRIAGE OF THE HOMEY ROAST CHICKEN AND THE EXOTIC
RICE PILAF MAKES THIS MENU FIT FOR THE MOST DISCERNING GUESTS.

KITCHENWARE: chef's knife, pepper mill, large saucepan with lid

PREPARATION TIME: 15 minutes

COOKING TIME: 25 minutes

2 TABLESPOONS SWEET BUTTER	$1/4$ TEASPOON DRIED CORIANDER
1 MEDIUM ONION, FINELY CHOPPED	$1/2$ TEASPOON SAFFRON THREADS
2 LARGE CLOVES GARLIC, MINCED	$1/8$ TEASPOON SALT
$1 1/2$ CUPS RAW WHITE RICE	$1/8$ TEASPOON FRESHLY GROUND PEPPER
$1/2$ CUP DICED DRIED APRICOTS	$3 1/3$ CUPS CHICKEN BROTH (FRESH OR CANNED, UNSALTED)
$1/2$ CUP RAISINS OR CURRANTS	
$1/2$ TEASPOON GROUND CINNAMON	

1. Heat the butter in the saucepan. Sauté the onion in the butter until slightly softened, 2 to 3 minutes. Add the garlic and sauté for 1 minute more. Add the rice and stir well, coating the grains until they are translucent.

2. Add the remaining ingredients. Bring to a simmer and stir gently. Cover the pan and cook over low heat until all the liquid is absorbed, about 18 to 20 minutes.

SERVICE: Let the pilaf stand covered for 5 minutes. Fluff the rice gently with a fork to blend all the ingredients. Serve the rice piping hot with the roast chicken.

COOK'S TIPS:

❖ If you have vegetarians coming for dinner, double the recipe and add toasted pecans or walnuts for both body and texture.

❖ Adding cooked chicken or lamb turns the pilaf into a fine main course.

Strawberry Shortcake Cream Puffs

THIS IS AN IRRESISTIBLE DESSERT THAT TURNS CALORIE COUNTERS AND CHOLESTEROL WATCHERS INTO GOOEY DESSERT LOVERS.

KITCHENWARE: small saucepan, wooden spoon, electric mixer with beater attachment and whisk attachment, baking sheet, cooling rack

PREPARATION TIME: 35 minutes

COOKING TIME: 2 minutes

BAKING TIME: 35 minutes

CREAM PUFFS:

2 1/2 TABLESPOONS SWEET BUTTER

1/2 CUP WATER

PINCH OF SALT

1 TEASPOON GRANULATED SUGAR

1/2 CUP FLOUR

2 EGGS, LIGHTLY BEATEN

FILLING:

1 PINT STRAWBERRIES

1 CUP HEAVY CREAM

1 TABLESPOON CONFECTIONERS' SUGAR

1 TEASPOON PURE VANILLA EXTRACT

1. Preheat the oven to 425 degrees.

2. To make the cream puffs, put the butter, water, salt, and sugar in the saucepan. Slowly bring the mixture to a boil. With the heat on high, add the flour all at once. Stir vigorously with a wooden spoon until the paste forms a ball and stands away from the sides of the pan. Cook for about 1 minute, gently stirring the ball.

3. Place the paste in the bowl of the electric mixer fitted with the beater attachment. Beat on low for 1 minute. This allows the steam to escape. Add the eggs, a little at a time, until the mixture is smooth and glossy.

4. For each puff (8 altogether), spoon 1 heaping tablespoon of the batter onto an ungreased baking sheet, allowing 1½ inches of space between puffs. Bake the cream puffs for 35 minutes. Gently tap the top of the puffs. If they sound hollow, they are done.

5. Cool the puffs on a rack for 10 minutes. Cut each cream puff in half horizontally to allow the moisture to escape.

6. While the puffs cool, make the filling. Wash, hull, and pat the strawberries dry. Cut them into ¼-inch slices.

   If the berries are large, cut each slice in half.

7. Just before serving, whip the cream, confectioners' sugar, and vanilla in the bowl of the electric mixer until the cream stands in firm peaks.

SERVICE: Fold the strawberries into the cream. Heap the bottom of each puff with the strawberry whipped cream filling. Gently place the top over the cream. Serve 2 puffs per person, with Raspberry Sauce (page 169).

COOK'S TIP: Unfilled cream puffs freeze beautifully. Keep extras on hand. Fill them with ice cream and serve to unexpected guests.

Cooking Together
The Roast Chicken Dinner

SEVERAL DAYS IN ADVANCE

COOK 1: STRAWBERRY SHORTCAKE CREAM PUFFS

Bake the cream puffs. Cool to room temperature. Freeze whole, well covered. Make the Raspberry Sauce (page 169) and refrigerate.

COOK 2: TURKISH RICE PILAF

Dice the apricots and measure the raisins, cinnamon, coriander, saffron, salt, and pepper. Mix in a small bowl and store, well covered, at room temperature.

THE NIGHT BEFORE

COOK 1: ROAST CHICKEN WITH ROOT VEGETABLES

Make the herbed butter. Place the herbed butter under and on top of the chicken skin (steps 2, 3, and 4). Prepare the onions, carrots, and turnip. Put the chicken on the bed of vegetables in the roasting pan, cover, and refrigerate.

COOK 2: CREAMY AVOCADO DRESSING

Chop the cilantro and red onion separately. Refrigerate each, covered. Make sure the avocados are ripe. If they do not feel perfectly ripe, take them out of the refrigerator and store at room temperature in a warm spot.

TURKISH RICE PILAF

Chop the onion and mince the garlic. Refrigerate each, covered.

THE MORNING OF THE DINNER

COOK 1: ORANGE, GRAPEFRUIT, AND AVOCADO SALAD

Prepare the oranges and grapefruit and arrange for service. Refrigerate, covered.

STRAWBERRY SHORTCAKE CREAM PUFFS

Transfer the cream puffs from the freezer to the refrigerator.

COOK 2: TURKISH RICE PILAF

Prepare the rice pilaf. Transfer the rice to an ovenproof casserole and store at room temperature, covered.

TOGETHER: Cut the berries for the cream puffs and refrigerate, covered. Prepare all the garnishes.

ONE HOUR BEFORE DINNER

COOK 1: ROAST CHICKEN WITH ROOT VEGETABLES

TURKISH RICE PILAF

Roast the chicken for 40 to 45 minutes at 400 degrees. Cover lightly with foil and leave in a 200-degree oven. If you have space while the chicken is roasting, reheat the rice for 25 minutes, or until it is piping hot. If space doesn't permit, put the rice in a 350-degree oven as soon as the chicken is finished. While the rice is heating, the chicken can stay at room temperature in a warm spot, lightly covered. If you have only one rack in the oven, balance the roasting pan over the casserole on the rack to keep both dishes hot before serving.

COOK 2: CREAMY AVOCADO DRESSING

Thirty minutes before serving, prepare the avocados for the salad. Make the Creamy Avocado Dressing. Drizzle the dressing over the fruit. Put extra dressing in a small bowl.

STRAWBERRY SHORTCAKE CREAM PUFFS

Make the whipped cream.

TOGETHER: Fill the cream puffs and refrigerate until dessert is served. Ready the sauce chosen for the dessert.

$$$

An Informal Barbecue

(ALL RECIPES SERVE 4)

MENU

TEQUILA GRILLED SHRIMP
WITH TEQUILA SUNSET TOMATO SAUCE

HONEY-GLAZED BARBECUED BABY BACK RIBS
WITH BROWN SUGAR BARBECUE SAUCE

CORN PUDDING

MARINATED FETA CHEESE, TOMATOES, AND RED ONION

PINEAPPLE UPSIDE-DOWN CAKE

SUGGESTED WINES: R. H. Phillips White Zinfandel, Dunnigan Hills, California

Girard Chenin Blanc, Napa Valley, California

McDowell Bistro Syrah, Mendocino County, California

A barbecue provides a delightful eating experience in a casual, laid-back setting.

In summer, you can barbecue on the beach, in the yard, on a boat, or in any safe spot you find to light up the coals. Dress warmly and you can even barbecue on a frosty winter night.

Whether it's hot dogs and hamburgers or shrimp and steak, the heady smell of burning coals and barbecue sauce combine to whet your guests' appetites. The clever host and hostess let their guests share in the grilling. There can never be too many cooks at a barbecue.

To create an informal table setting, use simple earthenware crockery and brightly colored napkins.

Don't forget an ice chest filled with soda and beer. Since many barbecues are "relax and get-your-fingers-dirty" capers, be sure to provide moist wipes for your guests!

Tequila Grilled Shrimp with Tequila Sunset Tomato Sauce

SHRIMP IS ALWAYS A TREAT. BARBECUED SHRIMP MARINATED IN A PIQUANT BLEND OF LIME JUICE, FRESH GINGER, AND TEQUILA IS TRULY A DELICACY.

KITCHENWARE: chef's knife, pepper mill, small steel mixing bowl, whisk, tongs, barbecue grill, self-starting charcoal, matches

PREPARATION TIME: 25 minutes (not including Tequila Sunset Tomato Sauce)

MARINATING TIME: 30 minutes

BARBECUE TIME: 4 minutes

¹/₄ CUP TEQUILA

¹/₂ CUP PEANUT OIL

¹/₄ CUP FRESH LIME JUICE (JUICE OF 1 LIME)

1 LARGE SHALLOT, FINELY MINCED

1 TABLESPOON FINELY MINCED FRESH GINGER

¹/₂ TEASPOON SALT

¹/₄ TEASPOON FRESHLY GROUND PEPPER

24 JUMBO RAW SHRIMP, PEELED, DEVEINED, TAILS LEFT ON

1 RECIPE TEQUILA SUNSET TOMATO SAUCE (RECIPE FOLLOWS)

GARNISH:

2 LIMES, QUARTERED

1. Light the coals 30 minutes before barbecuing, so that they are gray and glowing when you are ready to cook.

2. Whisk the tequila, peanut oil, lime juice, shallot, ginger, salt, and pepper in the mixing bowl.

3. Marinate the shrimp in this mixture for 30 minutes in the refrigerator.

   Do not marinate the shrimp for more than 30 minutes or the acid in the lime juice will start to break down the shrimp meat.

   Continued

While the shrimp marinates, make the tomato sauce.

4. Remove the shrimp from the marinade. Grill for 2 minutes on each side. As they cook, they will turn pink. The translucent center of the shrimp will become opaque. Serve immediately.

SERVICE: Serve 6 shrimp per person. Garnish with fresh lime. Serve with Tequila Sunset Tomato Sauce on the side.

COOK'S TIPS:

❖   Serve 8 shrimp per person if Tequila Grilled Shrimp is your only entrée.

❖   If you do not have a grill, use the broiler.

❖   We like our sauce loaded with lime juice and horseradish. Adjust the seasonings to satisfy your own taste buds.

❖   Try the sauce with chilled lobster, crabmeat, or oysters.

TEQUILA SUNSET TOMATO SAUCE

KITCHENWARE: chef's knife, medium saucepan, small mixing bowl

PREPARATION TIME: 10 minutes

COOKING TIME: 10 minutes

2 TABLESPOONS PEANUT OIL

1 MEDIUM ONION, FINELY MINCED

1 ¼ CUPS TOMATO KETCHUP

2 TABLESPOONS FRESH LIME JUICE

1 TEASPOON DRAINED GRATED WHITE HORSERADISH

1 TEASPOON FINELY MINCED FRESH GINGER

1 TABLESPOON TEQUILA

1. Heat the oil in the saucepan. Sauté the onion until soft, about 3 minutes. Add the ketchup and simmer for 7 minutes.

2. Mix the lime juice, horseradish, ginger, and tequila in the mixing bowl. Add the onion and ketchup and chill the sauce.

MAKES 1 CUP

Honey-Glazed Barbecued Baby Back Ribs with Brown Sugar Barbecue Sauce

IT'S HARD TO TELL WHICH IS MORE ENJOYABLE: MUNCHING ON THE RIBS OR LICKING THE
EXCESS DRIPPINGS FROM OUR FINGERS! IT'S ALL PART OF THE INFORMALITY AND
FUN OF BARBECUING. REMEMBER TO HAVE A GOOD SUPPLY OF
EXTRA-LARGE NAPKINS AND MOIST WIPES ON HAND.

KITCHENWARE: chef's knife, large mixing bowl, whisk, stainless-steel or Pyrex roasting pan, barbecue grill, self-starting charcoal, matches, tongs, pastry brush

PREPARATION TIME: 15 minutes (not including Brown Sugar Barbecue Sauce)

MARINATING TIME: 2 hours (or overnight)

GRILLING TIME: 25 minutes

1 SMALL ONION, FINELY CHOPPED

2 CLOVES GARLIC, FINELY MINCED

1/4 CUP HONEY

1/2 TEASPOON CAYENNE

1 TEASPOON GROUND CUMIN

2/3 CUP VEGETABLE OIL

1/4 CUP DRY RED WINE

4 RACKS OF BABY BACK RIBS

1 RECIPE WARM BROWN SUGAR BARBECUE SAUCE (RECIPE FOLLOWS)

1. Light the coals about 30 minutes before barbecuing, so that they are gray and glowing when you are ready to cook.

Continued

2. Combine the onion, garlic, honey, cayenne, cumin, oil, and wine in the mixing bowl. Place the ribs in the marinade and coat both sides well. Marinate in the refrigerator, covered, for at least 2 hours (or overnight), turning the ribs occasionally.

3. While the ribs marinate make the barbecue sauce.

4. Remove the ribs from the marinade and grill over gray coals for 15 minutes. While the ribs are cooking, baste the top side with warm Brown Sugar Barbecue Sauce. Turn the ribs and grill for 10 minutes on the other side; brush the cooked side with the barbecue sauce. The ribs are done when the juices run clear.

SERVICE: Serve 1 rack per person. Pass the additional Brown Sugar Barbecue Sauce. If you are serving just ribs, serve 2 racks per person.

COOK'S TIPS:

❖ Baby back ribs are smaller than regular spare ribs and, therefore, cook faster. Cover larger ribs with Brown Sugar Barbecue Sauce and roast them first in the oven for 20 minutes. Finish the ribs on the grill.

❖ Don't hesitate to serve this sauce with barbecued lamb or chicken.

BROWN SUGAR BARBECUE SAUCE

KITCHENWARE: chef's knife, pepper mill, medium sauté pan

PREPARATION TIME: 15 minutes

COOKING TIME: 15 minutes

2 TABLESPOONS VEGETABLE OIL	1 TABLESPOON WORCESTERSHIRE SAUCE
1 MEDIUM ONION, FINELY CHOPPED	3 TABLESPOONS BROWN SUGAR
2 CLOVES GARLIC, FINELY MINCED	3 TABLESPOONS CIDER VINEGAR
1 1/2 CUPS TOMATO SAUCE	SALT AND FRESHLY GROUND PEPPER
2 TEASPOONS DIJON MUSTARD	

1. Heat the oil in the sauté pan. Sauté the onion until soft, about 3 minutes. Add the garlic and sauté for 1 minute more.

2. Add the remaining ingredients. Simmer for 10 minutes.

MAKES 1 1/2 CUPS

Corn Pudding

CORN PUDDING ISN'T JUST FOR BARBECUES. THINK OF IT ANY TIME AS A
WONDERFUL SUBSTITUTE FOR POTATOES OR RICE.

KITCHENWARE: chef's knife, pepper mill, pastry brush, medium casserole, medium saucepan, food processor, electric mixer with whisk, large roasting pan, cake tester

PREPARATION TIME: 25 minutes

BAKING TIME: 1 hour

1 PINT HEAVY CREAM

3 CUPS FROZEN CORN KERNELS, THAWED

1/3 CUP YELLOW CORNMEAL

3 TABLESPOONS FLOUR

3/4 TEASPOON GROUND CUMIN

1 TEASPOON SALT

1/4 TEASPOON CAYENNE

1/3 TEASPOON FRESHLY GROUND BLACK PEPPER

6 EGGS

1/2 CUP DICED ROASTED RED BELL PEPPERS (JARRED)

3/4 CUP DICED SCALLIONS (WHITE AND GREEN PARTS)

1. Preheat the oven to 375 degrees. Lightly brush the inside of the casserole with vegetable oil.

2. Scald the cream by bringing it to a boil in the saucepan; immediately remove the pan from the heat.

3. Puree 2 cups of the corn in the food processor.

4. In the electric mixer, combine the cornmeal, flour, cumin, salt, cayenne, and black pepper. Add the eggs and beat the mixture until well blended. Slowly add the scalded cream and blend the mixture for 1 minute.

5. Add the pureed corn, the remaining cup of whole corn kernels, the roasted red bell peppers, and the scallions. Mix until all the ingredients are well combined. Pour the mixture into the prepared casserole.

Continued

6. Place the casserole in the roasting pan in the oven. Add hot water to the pan halfway up the outside of the casserole. Bake for about 50 minutes to 1 hour, until a tester placed in the center comes out clean and the top is toasty brown.

SERVICE: The Corn Pudding can be served hot right from the baking dish or at room temperature.

COOK'S TIPS:

❖ In the summer, when young sweet corn is in season, scrape the kernels from 9 medium ears of corn, blanch them, and substitute for the frozen variety.

❖ If the top of the pudding browns too quickly, cover the top with foil until it sets.

❖ Add 1 cup diced smoked ham to the Corn Pudding for an unusual main course.

Marinated Feta Cheese, Tomatoes, and Red Onion

THIS SALAD IS AT ITS BEST IN SUMMER WHEN THE TOMATOES ARE RIPE AND SUCCULENT.

KITCHENWARE: chef's knife, pepper mill, medium mixing bowl

PREPARATION TIME: 15 minutes

MARINATING TIME: 30 minutes

4 OUNCES FETA CHEESE

¹/₂ CUP VIRGIN OLIVE OIL

3 TABLESPOONS FRESH LEMON JUICE

¹/₂ TEASPOON RED PEPPER FLAKES

¹/₂ TEASPOON FRESHLY GROUND BLACK PEPPER

1 TEASPOON FINELY CHOPPED FRESH OREGANO

1 TEASPOON FINELY CHOPPED FRESH THYME

3 BEEFSTEAK TOMATOES

1 LARGE RED ONION

GARNISH:

¹/₂ CUP NIÇOISE OLIVES

2 FRESH THYME SPRIGS

1. Break the cheese into ¹/₄-inch cubes in the mixing bowl. Toss with ¹/₄ cup of the olive oil, 2 tablespoons of the lemon juice, the red pepper flakes, black pepper, oregano, and thyme. Marinate at room temperature for 30 minutes (or for up to 3 days, covered, in the refrigerator), and drain well. If refrigerated, bring to room temperature before assembling the salad.

2. Cut each tomato into four ¹/₂-inch slices. Cut the onion into ¹/₈-inch slices.

SERVICE: Mound the marinated cheese in the center of a serving platter. Surround the cheese with overlapping slices of tomato. Separate the onion slices into rings. Scatter onion rings and olives over the tomatoes. Drizzle with the remaining olive oil and lemon juice and decorate with the sprigs of thyme.

Pineapple Upside-Down Cake

IT'S THE SWEET THINGS IN LIFE THAT WE REMEMBER. THE AROMA OF PINEAPPLE UPSIDE-DOWN
CAKE TRANSPORTS US BACK TO OUR CHILDHOOD. THIS SCRUMPTIOUS CAKE IS A
FITTING END TO A HOMEY, INFORMAL BARBECUE.

KITCHENWARE: grater, 4 individual ramekins, waxed paper, rubber spatula, electric mixer with whisk attachment, small mixing bowl, cake tester, small saucepan, pastry brush

PREPARATION TIME: 20 minutes

BAKING TIME: 25 minutes

COOKING TIME: 2 minutes

4 WHOLE SLICES CANNED PINEAPPLE, DRAINED

8 TABLESPOONS (1 STICK) SWEET BUTTER, SOFTENED

3/4 CUP SUGAR

2 LARGE EGGS, AT ROOM TEMPERATURE

2 TEASPOONS PURE VANILLA EXTRACT

1 TABLESPOON PLUS 1/2 TEASPOON BRANDY

GRATED ZEST OF 1 LEMON

1 1/2 CUPS FLOUR

1 1/2 TEASPOONS BAKING POWDER

1/2 CUP PINEAPPLE OR APRICOT PRESERVES

GARNISH:

4 FRESH CHERRIES OR DRAINED CANNED CHERRIES

1. Preheat the oven to 350 degrees.

2. Butter 4 individual ramekins. Line the bottom of each ramekin with a circle of waxed paper and butter the paper. Place 1 pineapple slice on the bottom of each ramekin.

3. With the electric mixer on medium, beat the butter and sugar until light and fluffy, scraping down the sides of the bowl a few times. Add the eggs, vanilla, 1 tablespoon of the brandy, and the lemon zest. Blend until smooth.

The cake batter has a dense pound-cake-like consistency. For a lighter cake, separate the eggs. Add only the egg yolks in step 3. Whip the whites and fold them into the batter after adding the flour to the egg yolk mixture in step 4.

4. Combine the flour and baking powder and slowly add to the batter. Spoon the batter over each pineapple slice.

5. Bake the cakes for 20 to 25 minutes, until the tester comes out clean. Cool the ramekins for 10 minutes. Run a knife between the ramekin and the cake, tap lightly on the bottom, and unmold the cakes upside down. Peel off the waxed paper.

6. Melt the preserves with the remaining $^1/_2$ teaspoon of the brandy in the saucepan. Brush this glaze over the pineapple slices.

SERVICE: Place one cherry in the center of each slice of pineapple.

COOK'S TIPS:

❖ If the glaze cools down, reheat it before brushing over the cakes.

❖ Store leftover cakes in the refrigerator in a covered plastic container. Rebrush with warm glaze before serving.

Cooking Together
An Informal Barbecue

SEVERAL DAYS IN ADVANCE

COOK 1: **TEQUILA GRILLED SHRIMP**

TEQUILA SUNSET TOMATO SAUCE

Make the shrimp marinade and refrigerate, covered. Make the Tequila Sunset Tomato Sauce, but do not add the tequila. Add the tequila the day of the barbecue.

MARINATED FETA CHEESE, TOMATOES, AND RED ONION

Cube and marinate the feta cheese and refrigerate, covered.

COOK 2: **HONEY-GLAZED BARBECUED BABY BACK RIBS**

BROWN SUGAR BARBECUE SAUCE

Prepare baby back rib marinade and refrigerate, covered. Prepare the Brown Sugar Barbecue Sauce, cool to room temperature, and refrigerate, covered.

THE NIGHT BEFORE

COOK 1: **MARINATED FETA CHEESE, TOMATOES, AND RED ONION**

Slice the onion and refrigerate, covered.

PINEAPPLE UPSIDE-DOWN CAKE

Prepare the ramekins for the cakes. Store in the refrigerator.

COOK 2: **CORN PUDDING**

Puree the corn and refrigerate, covered. Combine the cornmeal, flour, cumin, salt, cayenne, and black pepper in a small bowl. Store at room temperature. Prepare the roasted red bell peppers and scallions. Refrigerate, covered.

TOGETHER: Marinate the baby back ribs and refrigerate. Buy the charcoal and matches.

THE MORNING OF THE BARBECUE

COOK 1:   CORN PUDDING

Bake the Corn Pudding and store at room temperature in a cool place.

PINEAPPLE UPSIDE-DOWN CAKE

As soon as the pudding is finished, bake and glaze the cakes. Store at room temperature.

COOK 2:   TEQUILA GRILLED SHRIMP

TEQUILA SUNSET TOMATO SAUCE

Bring the shrimp marinade to room temperature. Add the tequila to the tomato sauce and reseason.

MARINATED FETA CHEESE, TOMATOES, AND RED ONION

Slice the tomatoes and arrange the salad. Do not drizzle with the dressing.

TOGETHER: Prepare the garnishes.

ONE HOUR BEFORE THE BARBECUE

COOK 1:   TEQUILA GRILLED SHRIMP

Thirty minutes before the barbecue, light the coals and marinate the shrimp.

HONEY-GLAZED BARBECUED BABY BACK RIBS

Remove the ribs from the refrigerator and bring to room temperature.

BROWN SUGAR BARBECUE SAUCE

If serving the barbecue sauce warm, heat in the top of a stainless-steel double boiler. Reseason to taste.

COOK 2: CORN PUDDING

Reheat the Corn Pudding in a water bath in a 350-degree oven until warm, about 25 minutes.

PINEAPPLE UPSIDE-DOWN CAKE

Reglaze the cakes.

MARINATED FETA CHEESE, TOMATOES, AND RED ONION

Drizzle with the dressing and garnish.

TOGETHER: Let's barbecue!

$$

A Howling Halloween

(ALL RECIPES SERVE 4)

MENU

CRABBY CRAB CAKES WITH CILANTRO SOUR CREAM SAUCE

SORCERER'S CHEESY LASAGNA

"RED HOT" CHUNKY APPLESAUCE

MERRILY MARINATED VEGETABLE BREAD

TRICK-OR-TREAT CANDY CORN ICE CREAM CAKES

DUNKING-FOR-APPLES CIDER

SUGGESTED WINES: R. H. Phillips Chardonnay, Dunnigan Hills, California
Rex Hill Pinot Noir "King Ridge," Willamette, Oregon

How about a costume party for your "first" Halloween together? Invite a favorite couple to join you. Local variety stores are filled with inexpensive decorating ideas to make you look like a professional party planner.

Make a centerpiece with ghosts, goblins, and witches popping out of a pumpkin. Add small orange candles and eerie lighting to set the scene for this mischievous menu.

With the excitement of dressing up in costumes, your friends will arrive with the expectation of fun and intrigue. Your evening will be a success before the first morsel of food has been swallowed. The trick, of course, is for you to have fun too. Our menu, reflecting the colors and tastes of Halloween, allows you to enjoy the evening, since everything can be prepared in advance.

Crabby Crab Cakes with Cilantro Sour Cream Sauce

CRAB CAKES ARE A WELCOME ADDITION TO ANY MENU—AS A BITE-SIZE HORS D'OEUVRE, A LIGHT LUNCH, OR A HEARTY DINNER. THIS RECIPE IS ONE OF OUR FAVORITES.

KITCHENWARE: chef's knife, pepper mill, medium mixing bowl, waxed paper, medium sauté pan, paper toweling, baking sheet

PREPARATION TIME: 30 minutes (not including Cilantro Sour Cream Sauce)

COOKING TIME: 2 minutes

BAKING TIME: 10 minutes

1 EGG, BEATEN

2 TEASPOONS FRESH LEMON JUICE

2 TABLESPOONS MAYONNAISE

2 TABLESPOONS FINELY DICED RED BELL PEPPER

2 TABLESPOONS FINELY DICED RED ONION

1 TABLESPOON CHOPPED FRESH CILANTRO

1/8 TEASPOON SALT

FRESHLY GROUND BLACK PEPPER

DASH OF CAYENNE

1/2 POUND FRESH CRABMEAT, PICKED CLEAN OF SHELL AND CARTILAGE

1 CUP DRY UNSEASONED BREAD CRUMBS

1 RECIPE CILANTRO SOUR CREAM SAUCE (RECIPE FOLLOWS)

4 TABLESPOONS CORN OIL

GARNISH:

8 LETTUCE CUPS, BOSTON OR FRISÉE

4 LEMON WEDGES

1. Put the egg, lemon juice, mayonnaise, red bell pepper, onion, cilantro, salt, black pepper, and cayenne into the mixing bowl and mix well. Add the crabmeat and half the bread crumbs. Blend well.

Continued

2. Form the seasoned crabmeat into eight 2-inch cakes and coat them on both sides with the remaining bread crumbs. Place the cakes on the waxed paper and put them in the freezer for 15 minutes.

3. Prepare the Cilantro Sour Cream Sauce while the cakes are in the freezer.

4. Preheat the oven to 350 degrees.

5. Heat half the oil in the sauté pan. Fry half the cakes on both sides, about 30 seconds on each side, until golden. Drain on paper toweling. Repeat with the remaining oil and cakes.

   The oil should be hot but not smoking.

6. Transfer the cakes to the baking sheet and bake for 10 minutes.

SERVICE: Put 2 lettuce cups on each plate. Place a crab cake in each cup and garnish with a lemon wedge in the center. Serve with Cilantro Sour Cream Sauce.

COOK'S TIPS:

❖ Prepare and refrigerate the crab cakes the day before. However, do not coat them with bread crumbs. Before frying, coat with bread crumbs and freeze for 15 minutes.

❖ Any cooked fish or shellfish can be substituted for the crabmeat. We like to combine shrimp, lobster, and crabmeat, form larger cakes, and serve them with a green salad.

CILANTRO SOUR CREAM SAUCE

KITCHENWARE: chef's knife, pepper mill, small bowl

PREPARATION TIME: 10 minutes

1/3 CUP MAYONNAISE

1 1/2 CUPS SOUR CREAM

1 TABLESPOON LEMON JUICE

2 TABLESPOONS FINELY DICED RED BELL PEPPER

1 CLOVE GARLIC, FINELY MINCED

1 TEASPOON FINELY CHOPPED FRESH CILANTRO

SALT AND FRESHLY GROUND PEPPER

Blend all the ingredients in the small bowl.

MAKES 2 CUPS

Sorcerer's Cheesy Lasagna

THIS LASAGNA, TOPPED WITH SHREDDED ORANGE CARROTS AND BLACK OLIVES, IS THE PERFECT CENTERPIECE FOR A COLORFUL HALLOWEEN DINNER.

KITCHENWARE: chef's knife, grater, vegetable peeler, pepper mill, large saucepan, colander, waxed paper, small mixing bowl, rubber spatula, $10 \times 6^{1}/_{2} \times 2$-inch baking dish, aluminum foil

PREPARATION TIME: 40 minutes

COOKING TIME: 12 minutes

BAKING TIME: 45 minutes

5 QUARTS WATER	1 CUP FRESHLY GRATED PARMESAN CHEESE
9 UNCOOKED LASAGNA STRIPS	12 OUNCES MOZZARELLA CHEESE, GRATED
3 TEASPOONS VIRGIN OLIVE OIL	$^{1}/_{4}$ TEASPOON SALT
3 CLOVES GARLIC, FINELY MINCED	$^{1}/_{4}$ TEASPOON FRESHLY GROUND PEPPER
ONE 10-OUNCE BOX FROZEN SPINACH, DEFROSTED AND SQUEEZED DRY	4 PLUM TOMATOES, CUT INTO $^{1}/_{8}$-INCH SLICES
15 OUNCES RICOTTA CHEESE	1 SMALL CARROT, PEELED, SHREDDED, AND CHOPPED
1 TABLESPOON FINELY CHOPPED FRESH BASIL LEAVES	$^{1}/_{4}$ CUP THINLY SLICED PITTED BLACK OLIVES
1 EGG	
1 CUP GRATED FONTINA CHEESE	

1. Preheat the oven to 375 degrees.

2. Bring the water to a boil in the large saucepan. Add the lasagna, a few strips at a time, stirring with each addition. Cook the pasta for 8 minutes. Drain and place each strip separately on the waxed paper to prevent the noodles from sticking together.

   Omit this step if using precooked lasagna strips, available in some markets.

   Continued

3. Heat 2 teaspoons of the olive oil in the same saucepan. Sauté the garlic for 30 seconds. Add the spinach and cook over moderate heat for 3 minutes.

4. Combine the ricotta cheese, spinach, basil, egg, $\frac{1}{2}$ cup of the Fontina cheese, $\frac{1}{2}$ cup of the Parmesan cheese, $\frac{1}{2}$ of the mozzarella cheese, the salt, and pepper in the mixing bowl.

5. Rub the baking dish with the remaining teaspoon of olive oil. Place 3 overlapping strips of lasagna on the bottom and add half the cheese mixture. Layer half the tomatoes over the cheese. Repeat with another layer of lasagna, cheese, and tomato. Top with the 3 remaining strips of pasta.

6. Mix the rest of the cheeses with the carrot and olives and sprinkle evenly over the noodles. Cover the lasagna with aluminum foil and bake for 35 minutes. Uncover and bake for 8 to 10 minutes more, until the cheeses are bubbly and golden brown.

Prepare the lasagna without the carrots and olives at other times of the year.

SERVICE: Let the lasagna stand for 10 minutes before serving. This allows the ingredients to settle and makes the lasagna easier to cut.

COOK'S TIPS:

❖ Double the lasagna recipe and bake in a $13 \times 9 \times 2$-inch baking dish. The preparation time will increase by about 15 minutes, the cooking time will remain the same.

❖ Put the lasagna together the day before and refrigerate unbaked. Bring it to room temperature before baking.

"Red Hot" Chunky Applesauce

THIS DELICIOUS SIDE DISH ADDS A TOUCH OF FIRE TO THE MELLOW

SORCERER'S CHEESY LASAGNA.

KITCHENWARE: apple corer, paring knife, medium saucepan with lid

PREPARATION TIME: 15 minutes

COOKING TIME: 11 minutes

4 GRANNY SMITH APPLES (ABOUT 2 POUNDS)

½ CUP ORANGE JUICE

1 CUP WHOLE CRANBERRIES

¼ CUP GRANULATED SUGAR

¼ CUP BROWN SUGAR

3 TABLESPOONS "RED HOT" CANDIES OR CINNAMON DECOR CANDY

1 TEASPOON PURE VANILLA EXTRACT

1. Peel and core the apples. Cut them into ¼-inch dice.

2. Bring the orange juice to a boil in the saucepan and add the apples, cranberries, sugars, and "red hot" candies.

3. Cook, covered, for 8 to 10 minutes, until the cranberries have popped and the apples are soft. Carefully blend in the vanilla.

SERVICE: Heap the chunky applesauce into glass or china compote dishes. Sprinkle a few "red hots" on top.

COOK'S TIPS:

- ❖ For a smoother applesauce, put the cooked fruit mixture into the food processor and pulse a few times.

- ❖ Substitute cinnamon to taste for the "red hots" for a less spicy, classic applesauce. Serve this classic version with seafood, roasts, chicken, or holiday dinner.

Merrily Marinated Vegetable Bread

KITCHENWARE: chef's knife, pepper mill, food processor, spatula, stainless-steel bowl, baking sheet

PREPARATION TIME: 30 minutes

MARINATING TIME: 4 hours

COOKING TIME: 5 minutes

MARINADE:

2 CLOVES GARLIC, PEELED

1 TEASPOON DIJON MUSTARD

$\frac{1}{4}$ TEASPOON FRESHLY GROUND PEPPER

$\frac{1}{8}$ TEASPOON SALT

1 TABLESPOON FRESH LEMON JUICE

2 TABLESPOONS BALSAMIC VINEGAR

$\frac{1}{3}$ CUP VIRGIN OLIVE OIL

VEGETABLES:

1 LARGE RED BELL PEPPER, DICED SMALL

1 MEDIUM ZUCCHINI, DICED SMALL

1 MEDIUM SUMMER SQUASH, DICED SMALL

$1\frac{1}{2}$ CUPS FINELY DICED MUSHROOMS

SALT AND FRESHLY GROUND PEPPER

ASSEMBLING THE BREAD:

1 FRENCH BREAD

1. To make the marinade, place the garlic, mustard, pepper, salt, lemon juice, and vinegar into the bowl of the food processor. Pulse a few times, until the garlic is minced. Scrape down the sides of the bowl between pulses to make sure all ingredients are processed evenly.

2. With the motor running, slowly pour the oil through the feed tube and process for 30 seconds. The marinade will have the consistency of beaten egg whites.

3. To prepare the vegetables, place them in the stainless-steel bowl and toss well with the marinade. Marinate the vegetables in the refrigerator for not more than 4 hours. Season with salt and pepper just before using.

4. Preheat the oven to 350 degrees and preheat the broiler.

If you cannot heat your broiler and oven at the same time, toast the bread under the broiler first. Then heat your oven, and finish the recipe.

5. Cut the French bread in half lengthwise. Open the 2 long halves, and cut each half into 4 pieces. Put the bread on the baking sheet and toast under the broiler until golden.

6. Spread the vegetables over the toasted bread and warm in the oven for 5 minutes.

SERVICE: Place the bread onto a napkin-lined flat basket.

COOK'S TIPS:

❖   The bread is splendid with grilled meats or fish.

❖   The marinade makes a zesty dressing for salads or cold pastas.

❖   The marinated vegetables can be doubled and served as part of an antipasto.

Trick-or-Treat Candy Corn Ice Cream Cakes

THESE ICE CREAM CAKES ARE A SPECIAL TREAT, REMINISCENT OF RINGING DOORBELLS, SHOUTS OF "TRICK OR TREAT," AND BAGS FILLED WITH CANDY CORN.

KITCHENWARE: food processor, small saucepan, 6-cup muffin pan, nonstick cooking spray, small bowl, ice cream scoop

PREPARATION TIME: 20 minutes

FREEZING TIME: 45 minutes

1 QUART VANILLA ICE CREAM (OR YOUR FAVORITE FLAVOR)

12 OREO COOKIES

¼ CUP (½ STICK) SWEET BUTTER, MELTED

¼ CUP HALVED CANDY CORN

GARNISH:

CANDY CORN

1.   Soften the ice cream for 10 minutes at room temperature.

2.   While the ice cream is softening, crush the Oreo cookies into crumbs in the bowl of the food processor. Blend the crumbs with the melted butter.

3.   Spray the muffin cups with nonstick cooking spray. Press half of the Oreo crumb mixture onto the bottoms of the muffin cups. Freeze for 5 minutes.

4.   Put the ice cream into a bowl and fold in the candy corn. Freeze the ice cream for 10 minutes.

    Work quickly so the ice cream does not melt.

5.   Scoop the ice cream into balls. Sprinkle the remaining Oreo crumbs onto a piece of waxed paper. Roll the balls in the crumbs and press into the muffin cups. Put the cakes into the freezer for 30 minutes.

SERVICE: Take the cakes out of the freezer 10 minutes before serving. Garnish the top of each cake with candy corn.

COOK'S TIP: Double the recipe and use a 12-cup muffin pan.

Dunking-for-Apples Cider

THIS CIDER REALLY PACKS A PUNCH. REMEMBER THE FORMULA WHEN YOU WANT TO TAKE THE CHILL OUT OF A WINTRY EVENING.

❧

KITCHENWARE: apple corer, paring knife, medium stainless-steel saucepan

PREPARATION TIME: 15 minutes

COOKING TIME: 25 minutes

1 QUART APPLE CIDER

6 OUNCES CALVADOS OR APPLE BRANDY

4 CINNAMON STICKS

4 WHOLE CLOVES

1 RED DELICIOUS APPLE, PEELED, CORED, AND DICED

1 GRANNY SMITH APPLE, PEELED, CORED, AND DICED

1 YELLOW DELICIOUS APPLE, PEELED, CORED, AND DICED

4 TEASPOONS COGNAC

GARNISH:

1 RED DELICIOUS APPLE, CORED AND CUT INTO $\frac{1}{2}$-INCH-THICK STICKS (SEE COOK'S TIP)

1. Put the cider, brandy, cinnamon sticks, and cloves into the saucepan. Bring to a boil and skim off any foam that may rise to the top. Simmer for 15 minutes.

2. Add the diced apples and simmer 10 minutes more.

SERVICE: Put 1 teaspoon of Cognac in each punch cup. Add the hot cider and garnish with the apple sticks.

COOK'S TIP: Toss the apples in lemon juice and drain to keep them white.

Cooking Together
A Howling Halloween

SEVERAL DAYS IN ADVANCE

COOK 1: SORCERER'S CHEESY LASAGNA

Grate the Fontina, Parmesan, and mozzarella cheeses and mince the garlic. Seal tightly in plastic wrap and refrigerate (the cheeses can be stored together, the garlic separately).

MERRILY MARINATED VEGETABLE BREAD

Make the marinade and refrigerate, covered.

COOK 2: "RED HOT" CHUNKY APPLESAUCE

Make the applesauce and refrigerate, covered.

TOGETHER: TRICK-OR-TREAT CANDY CORN ICE CREAM CAKES

Make and freeze as directed. Don't garnish before freezing.

THE NIGHT BEFORE

COOK 1: CRABBY CRAB CAKES WITH CILANTRO SOUR CREAM SAUCE

Prepare and form the crab cakes. Do not coat them with the remaining bread crumbs at this time. (The bread crumbs will become too moist in the refrigerator.) Make the sauce, *leaving out the cilantro*. Refrigerate, covered.

COOK 2: SORCERER'S CHEESY LASAGNA

Make the lasagna steps 2 through 5. Cool the noodles and spinach to room temperature and refrigerate, lightly covered.

TOGETHER: DUNKING-FOR-APPLES CIDER

Make the cider and refrigerate, covered.

Halloween Morning

Cook 1: Merrily Marinated Vegetable Bread

Cut and toast the French bread. Dice and marinate the vegetables. (Don't marinate for more than 4 hours before using.)

Sorcerer's Cheesy Lasagna

Bring back to room temperature in a cool spot in the kitchen. Prepare the carrots and olives and garnish the top as directed.

Cook 2: Crabby Crab Cakes

Line the crab cake plates with the lettuce cups and refrigerate. Slice the lemon wedges.

Dunking-for-Apples Cider

Fill the punch cups with Cognac.

One Hour Before

Cook 1: Crabby Crab Cakes with Cilantro Sour Cream Sauce

Preheat the oven. Coat the crab cakes with the bread crumbs and complete the recipe. Place the baked crab cakes in a warm place in the kitchen. Bring the sauce to room temperature, add the cilantro, and correct the seasonings.

Dunking-for-Apples Cider

Prepare the apple sticks and warm the cider.

Cook 2: Sorcerer's Cheesy Lasagna

Bake the lasagna as soon as the crab cakes are finished.

Merrily Marinated Vegetable Bread

Spread the vegetables on the French Bread. Heat in the oven as soon as the lasagna is finished.

Together: Trick-or-Treat Candy Corn Ice Cream Cakes

Take the ice cream cakes out of the freezer 10 minutes before serving dessert. Garnish the tops with candy corn.

$$

Fondue Frenzy

(ALL RECIPES SERVE 4)

MENU

RED WINE–MARINATED BEEF FONDUE

MUSTARD SAUCE

TERIYAKI SAUCE

GREEN AND RED SALSA

VEGETABLE-CHEESE TART

SPINACH, ASPARAGUS, AND ONION SALAD

CHOCOLATE-KAHLÚA FONDUE WITH FRESH FRUIT AND ALMOND-ESPRESSO CAKE

SUGGESTED WINES: McDowell Grenache Rosé, Mendocino County, California
Buena Vista Pinot Noir, Sonoma County, California

FONDUE, ONE OF OUR MOST FAVORITE FOODS, IS IN VOGUE AGAIN! FONDUE EQUIPMENT IS A

WELCOME GIFT AT ANY BRIDAL SHOWER. WHETHER YOU CHOOSE CHEESE, SEAFOOD, BEEF,

OR CHOCOLATE, FONDUE IS DELICIOUS, FUN TO PREPARE, AND BEST OF ALL, A GROUP

ACTIVITY. THERE CERTAINLY IS A GREAT DEAL OF FOOD PREPARATION FOR YOUR FEAST,

BUT THE GOOD NEWS IS, IT CAN ALL BE DONE AHEAD. FORTUNATELY, YOUR GUESTS

DO THE LAST-MINUTE COOKING, ENABLING YOU TO RELAX AND ENJOY YOUR OWN PARTY.

THIS IS A PERFECT SUPPER TO SERVE AFTER A FIVE O'CLOCK SUNDAY MOVIE, AN

AFTERNOON OF GALLERY BROWSING, OR JUST AN OLD-FASHIONED

REUNION WITH FRIENDS.

THE FOCUS OF THE TABLE SETTING SHOULD BE ON THE COOKING. SOLID PLATES

(ESPECIALLY WHITE) ENHANCE THE COLORS OF THE FOODS TO BE DIPPED. THIS IS ALSO A

WONDERFUL TIME TO USE THOSE BIZARRE, ONE-OF-A-KIND BOWLS YOU RECEIVED AS

SHOWER AND WEDDING GIFTS. FILL THEM WITH THE THREE DIPPING SAUCES.

Red Wine–Marinated Beef Fondue

RED WINE GIVES A DELIGHTFUL FULL-BODIED TASTE TO A CLASSIC BEEF FONDUE.

KITCHENWARE: chef's knife, pepper mill, small bowl, medium saucepan, deep-frying thermometer, slotted spoon, fondue pot, 4 fondue forks

PREPARATION TIME: 20 minutes

MARINATING TIME: 2 hours

¹/₃ CUP VIRGIN OLIVE OIL

¹/₂ CUP RED TABLE WINE

1 MEDIUM ONION, FINELY CHOPPED

2 CLOVES GARLIC, MINCED

¹/₂ TEASPOON CHOPPED FRESH TARRAGON

¹/₄ TEASPOON FRESHLY GROUND PEPPER

2 POUNDS BONELESS SIRLOIN STEAK, CUT INTO 1¹/₂-INCH CUBES

4 CUPS VEGETABLE OIL (OR PEANUT OIL)

GARNISH:

¹/₂ BUNCH FLAT-LEAF PARSLEY

1. Combine the olive oil, wine, onion, garlic, tarragon, and pepper in the small bowl.

2. Put the steak cubes into the bowl and marinate for 2 hours or overnight in the refrigerator.

3. Heat the vegetable oil in the saucepan until the temperature on a deep-frying thermometer reaches 375 degrees. Fill the fondue pot with the oil just before serving.

   The oil must be hot enough for the beef to cook as soon as it is dipped into the fondue pot. To test, dip a small piece of beef into the oil; if it sizzles, the oil is ready. Handle hot oil with great care; spilled oil can catch fire. Table salt acts as a fire extinguisher when poured over a small fire.

SERVICE: Remove the beef from the marinade with a slotted spoon and divide the beef into 4 portions. Place 1 portion on each dinner plate. Surround with Mustard Sauce, Teriyaki Sauce, and Green and Red Salsa (pages 258–260) in individual bowls, or fill 3 large bowls with the sauces and put them in the middle of the table.

COOK'S TIP: If the temperature of the oil is correct, the beef will char on the outside and be pink on the inside. If the oil is too hot, over 375 degrees, it may cause the outside of the beef cubes to dry out.

Mustard Sauce

KITCHENWARE: chef's knife, pepper mill, small bowl

PREPARATION TIME: 5 minutes

1 CUP SOUR CREAM

1 1/2 TEASPOONS GRATED WHITE
HORSERADISH, DRAINED

1 TEASPOON DIJON MUSTARD

1 TEASPOON TARRAGON VINEGAR

1 CLOVE GARLIC, MINCED

SALT AND FRESHLY GROUND PEPPER

Combine the first 5 ingredients in the bowl and season with salt and pepper.

MAKES 1 1/4 CUPS

COOK'S TIP: Mustard Sauce is also ideal with grilled salmon, roasted lamb, and pork.

Teriyaki Sauce

KITCHENWARE: chef's knife, grater, pepper mill, small bowl

PREPARATION TIME: 10 minutes

¹/₂ CUP SOY SAUCE	**¹/₂ TEASPOON SESAME OIL**
3 TABLESPOONS FINELY MINCED ONION	**¹/₂ TEASPOON SESAME SEEDS**
¹/₂ TEASPOON GRATED FRESH GINGER	**FRESHLY GROUND PEPPER**

Combine the first 5 ingredients in the bowl, blend well, and season with pepper.

Prepare the sauce ahead of time. It will keep in the refrigerator for up to 1 week.

MAKES ³/₄ CUP

COOK'S TIP: The flavors of Teriyaki Sauce also enrich grilled pork, lamb, chicken, and tuna fish.

Green and Red Salsa

KITCHENWARE: chef's knife, small bowl

PREPARATION TIME: 20 minutes

1 SMALL GREEN BELL PEPPER, SEEDED
AND FINELY CHOPPED

1 TOMATO, SEEDED AND DICED

¼ CUP FINELY CHOPPED RED ONION

1 MEDIUM CLOVE GARLIC, MINCED

2 TEASPOONS MINCED SERRANO CHILI

2 TEASPOONS CHOPPED FRESH CILANTRO

1 TEASPOON RED WINE VINEGAR

¼ CUP TOMATO SAUCE

SALT

Combine the first 8 ingredients in the bowl and season with salt.

Plan to make the salsa the day before to give the seasonings time to blend and the flavors time to intensify.

MAKES 1 CUP

COOK'S TIP: This is the basic recipe for any dish that calls for salsa.

Vegetable-Cheese Tart

THE VIBRANT COLORS AND PIQUANT TASTE OF THE VEGETABLE CHEESE TART MAKE A
WONDERFUL SIDE DISH WITH THE FONDUE. THE INGREDIENTS CAN BE DOUBLED AND SERVED AS
A SATISFYING VEGETARIAN ENTRÉE. ADD A CRISP GREEN SALAD AND HEARTY
WARM BREAD TO COMPLETE THE MENU.

KITCHENWARE: chef's knife, grater, pepper mill, 2 baking sheets, spatula, small bowl, pastry brush

PREPARATION TIME: 25 minutes

BAKING TIME: 25 minutes

2 SMALL ZUCCHINI

2 SMALL YELLOW SQUASH

4 PLUM TOMATOES

¾ CUP RICOTTA CHEESE

4 OUNCES UNSEASONED GOAT CHEESE

¼ CUP FRESHLY GRATED PARMESAN CHEESE

4 TABLESPOONS PESTO, OR 1 TABLESPOON CHOPPED FRESH BASIL

SALT AND FRESHLY GROUND PEPPER

2 SHEETS PUFF PASTRY, DEFROSTED IN THE REFRIGERATOR

2 TABLESPOONS VIRGIN OLIVE OIL

GARNISH:

FRESH BASIL LEAVES

1. Preheat the oven to 400 degrees. Brush the baking sheets with olive oil and sprinkle with salt and pepper.

2. Slice the zucchini, squash, and tomatoes into ⅛-inch-thick rounds.

3. Blend the 3 cheeses, the pesto, ¼ teaspoon salt, and ¼ teaspoon pepper in the small bowl, until creamy.

   Pesto and puff pastry are available in the frozen food section of most food markets.

Continued

4. With the tip of a sharp knife, cut the puff pastry into four 6-inch rounds. Place two rounds on each baking sheet.

   You will have to re-form your pastry for 2 of the circles. Keep the pastry cold; chilled dough is easier to work with.

5. Spread the cheese mixture over the pastry rounds, leaving a 1-inch border. Arrange the zucchini, squash, and tomatoes over the cheese, in tight overlapping slices, alternating the vegetables.

6. Lightly brush the vegetables with the olive oil and sprinkle with salt and pepper. Bake the tarts for 25 minutes, until the pastry is golden and the vegetables are cooked through.

SERVICE: Serve the tarts warm, garnished with fresh basil leaves.

COOK'S TIPS:

❖ The tarts can be assembled in advance and refrigerated before baking.

❖ Serve the tarts as a first course with a meat, poultry, or fish entrée.

❖ The tarts travel well and are a welcome addition to any pot-luck party.

Spinach, Asparagus, and ✪nion Salad

YEARS AGO, SERVING FRESH SPINACH WAS A CHORE. REMOVING THE GRITTY SAND FROM

THE LEAVES WAS SO TIME-CONSUMING. TODAY, MARKETS ARE FULL OF FINE-QUALITY

SPINACH, ALREADY WASHED AND READY TO SERVE.

KITCHENWARE: chef's knife, pepper mill, large salad bowl, small saucepan, colander, 2 small bowls, whisk

PREPARATION TIME: 30 minutes

COOKING TIME: 3 minutes

$^1/_2$ POUND FRESH SPINACH, TRIMMED AND CLEANED

2 CUPS WATER

16 MEDIUM ASPARAGUS SPEARS, WASHED AND TRIMMED

3 TEASPOONS DIJON MUSTARD

$^1/_4$ CUP TARRAGON VINEGAR

$^1/_2$ CUP VIRGIN OLIVE OIL OR VEGETABLE OIL

$^1/_2$ TEASPOON SUGAR

SALT AND FRESHLY GROUND PEPPER

1 RED ONION, CUT INTO $^1/_8$-INCH-THICK SLICES

$^1/_2$ POUND WHITE MUSHROOMS

1 TEASPOON FRESH LEMON JUICE

1. Put the spinach leaves into a large salad bowl.

2. Bring the water to a boil. Blanch the asparagus for 3 minutes, drain, and immediately run under cold water to stop further cooking. Add the asparagus to the spinach.

3. Whisk the mustard, vinegar, oil, and sugar in a bowl. Season with salt and pepper. Separate the onion slices and put them into the dressing for 15 minutes.

4. Wash the mushrooms and pat dry (unless they are free from soil).

   Look under the cap, where dirt likes to hide.

Continued

Cut the mushrooms into ⅛-inch-thick slices. Toss the mushrooms and lemon juice in a small bowl.

The acid in the juice keeps the mushrooms snow white.

SERVICE: Drain the mushrooms. Toss together the mushrooms, onion, vinaigrette, spinach, and asparagus. Be sure to coat all the spinach leaves.

COOK'S TIPS:

❖   Buy tender young spinach, since older spinach leaves tend to be tough.

❖   Add crisp bacon, ham, cooked chicken, cheese, or other greens to make the spinach salad into a satisfying main course. Don't forget the hot crusty bread.

Chocolate-Kahlúa Fondue with Fresh Fruit and Almond-Espresso Cake

CHOCOLATE FONDUE IS AMBROSIA TO A CHOCOHOLIC. TANTALIZINGLY RICH, THE FONDUE IS A PERFECT MEDIUM FOR THE FRUIT AND THE ALMOND-ESPRESSO CAKE.

KITCHENWARE: stainless-steel double boiler, small saucepan, whisk, chef's knife, rubber spatula, fondue pot, 4 fondue forks

PREPARATION TIME: 25 minutes (not including Almond-Espresso Cake)

COOKING TIME: 12 minutes

1 RECIPE ALMOND-ESPRESSO CAKE (RECIPE FOLLOWS)

½ POUND SEMISWEET CHOCOLATE

½ CUP HEAVY CREAM

1 TABLESPOON KAHLÚA LIQUEUR

1 TABLESPOON BRANDY

1 BANANA

1 PINT STRAWBERRIES

2 MANGOES

2 ORANGES

1. Prepare the cake and while it bakes, make the fondue.

2. Melt the chocolate in the top of the double boiler over simmering water for about 12 minutes.

3. Whisk the cream, liqueur, and brandy into the chocolate, until the ingredients are well blended.

4. Slice the banana into ½-inch rounds; hull and stem the strawberries; peel, pit, and quarter the mangoes; and peel and quarter the oranges.

Continued

Prepare the strawberries, mangoes, and oranges 1 hour ahead. Slice the banana just before serving the fondue.

SERVICE: Pour the fondue into the fondue pot. Cut the cake into 1$\frac{1}{2}$ × 1$\frac{1}{2}$-inch chunks. Arrange the cake and the fruit on 4 dessert plates.

We have 2 fondue sets, metal for the beef and ceramic for the chocolate. If you don't have 2 pots, you can substitute a small casserole set over a Sterno to keep the chocolate warm, and you won't have to wash the beef pot before serving dessert.

COOK'S TIPS:

❖   The chocolate fondue can be prepared ahead of time. To rewarm, slowly simmer the chocolate in the top of the double boiler.

❖   Substitute your favorite fresh fruits for the ones we suggest.

❖   If there is no time to bake the Almond-Espresso Cake, use buttery pound cake, available in all food markets.

❖   Almond-Espresso Cake can also be served with your favorite freshly cut fruits and topped with Orange Chantilly Cream (page 163) or with Raspberry Sauce (page 169).

❖   One of our favorites is to cut the cake in half, cover the bottom with sliced fruit or berries, and top with whipped cream. Replace the top half for a delicious shortcake.

❖   Store leftover cake in an airtight container at room temperature for up to 2 days.

ALMOND-ESPRESSO CAKE

KITCHENWARE: chopper, electric mixer with whisk attachment, medium mixing bowl, fine-mesh strainer or sifter, rubber spatula, 9-inch springform pan, cooling rack

PREPARATION TIME: 20 minutes

BAKING TIME: 25 minutes

4 LARGE EGGS, AT ROOM TEMPERATURE

$\frac{3}{4}$ CUP SUGAR

1 TEASPOON PURE VANILLA EXTRACT

1 TABLESPOON INSTANT ESPRESSO DISSOLVED IN $\frac{1}{3}$ CUP WATER

$\frac{3}{4}$ CUP PLUS 2 TABLESPOONS ALL-PURPOSE FLOUR

$\frac{1}{2}$ TEASPOON BAKING POWDER

$\frac{1}{2}$ CUP CHOPPED ALMONDS

5 TABLESPOONS SWEET BUTTER, MELTED AND COOLED TO ROOM TEMPERATURE

1. Preheat the oven to 350 degrees. Lightly grease a 9-inch springform pan.

2. Beat the eggs at high speed in the bowl of the electric mixer until foamy, about 30 seconds. Slowly add the sugar and beat at high speed for 7 minutes. The mixture will be thick and a pale lemon color. Add the vanilla and espresso and blend well.

3. Sift the flour with the baking powder. Fold the flour and nuts into the egg and sugar mixture. Gently fold in the melted butter.

4. Pour the batter into the springform pan. Bake for 25 minutes, or until the top of the cake bounces back to the touch. Cool the cake on a rack for 5 minutes. Release the catch on the springform pan, invert the cake onto the rack, and remove the bottom of the pan. Reverse the cake and cool.

Cooking Together
Fondue Frenzy

SEVERAL DAYS IN ADVANCE

COOK 1: **MUSTARD SAUCE**

TERIYAKI SAUCE

Prepare both sauces. Refrigerate, well covered.

ALMOND-ESPRESSO CAKE

Prepare and bake the cake. Cool, and store in an airtight container at room temperature. If made more than 2 days in advance, the cake can be stored in the freezer.

COOK 2: **RED WINE–MARINATED BEEF FONDUE**

Make the marinade and refrigerate, covered.

GREEN AND RED SALSA

Make the salsa and refrigerate, covered.

SPINACH, ASPARAGUS, AND ONION SALAD

Prepare the vinaigrette, *omitting the onion*. Refrigerate, covered.

THE NIGHT BEFORE

COOK 1: **RED WINE–MARINATED BEEF FONDUE**

Cube the beef and marinate, covered, in the refrigerator.

SPINACH, ASPARAGUS, AND ONION SALAD

Wash and trim the spinach and dry well. Refrigerate in a plastic bag. Trim the ends of the asparagus. Wash and dry well. Refrigerate the asparagus in a plastic bag. Slice the red onion as directed and refrigerate, covered.

ALMOND-ESPRESSO CAKE

Transfer the cake from the freezer to the refrigerator.

COOK 2: VEGETABLE-CHEESE TART

Prepare the recipe steps 2 through 5. Refrigerate, covered.

THE MORNING OF THE FONDUE PARTY

COOK 1: MUSTARD AND TERIYAKI SAUCES AND SALSA

Correct the seasonings in the sauces and the salsa and replace in the refrigerator. (The salsa may accumulate some liquid from the vegetables. If it is too runny, pour off the excess before reseasoning.)

COOK 2: CHOCOLATE-KAHLÚA FONDUE

ALMOND-ESPRESSO CAKE

Make the chocolate dipping sauce (steps 1 and 2) and refrigerate, covered. Cut the cake into serving pieces and store in an airtight container at room temperature.

TOGETHER: Prepare all garnishes and assemble your fondue equipment.

ONE HOUR BEFORE

COOK 1: CHOCOLATE-KAHLÚA FONDUE

Prepare the strawberries, mangoes, and oranges.

RED WINE–MARINATED BEEF FONDUE

Arrange the beef on the dinner plates. Heat the oil over a low flame. Place the fondue sauces and salsa in serving bowls.

COOK 2: VEGETABLE-CHEESE TART

Preheat the oven and complete steps 1 and 6.

SPINACH, ASPARAGUS, AND ONION SALAD

Put the onion in the vinaigrette, as directed. Wash the mushrooms, as directed, and toss with the lemon juice.

CHOCOLATE-KAHLÚA FONDUE

Reheat the chocolate sauce in the top of a stainless-steel double boiler and taste for flavor. Since Kahlúa "cooks away" when heated, you may want to add more.

TOGETHER: Toss the salad. Make sure the oil is hot enough for the beef fondue. Slice the banana and brush it with lemon juice.

$$$

The Dinner Party

(ALL RECIPES SERVE 4)

MENU

AUTUMN ROOT VEGETABLE BISQUE

ROSEMARY-ROASTED RACK OF LAMB WITH CABERNET WINE SAUCE

NEW POTATOES WITH BALSAMIC VINEGAR GLAZE

SAUTÉED SPINACH AND LEEKS

VANILLA BEAN CRÈME BRÛLÉE

SUGGESTED WINES: Huntington Cabernet Sauvignon, Sonoma County, California

Laurel Glen Cabernet Sauvignon "Terra Rose," Napa Valley, California

Jordan Chardonnay, Sonoma County, California

AH YES, THERE ARE THOSE OF US WHO ARE GIFTED WITH THE INSTINCTIVE ABILITY TO COOK, BAKE, AND HAVE A GOLDEN PALATE. NOTHING IS TOO DIFFICULT; IN FACT, THE FEARLESS AMONG US THINK NOTHING OF TRYING OUT NEW RECIPES FOR OUR GUESTS. I FALL INTO THIS CATEGORY OF COOKS, AND I REMEMBER THE LEMON-SCENTED OSSO BUCCO AND SAFFRON RICE THAT FIRMLY ESTABLISHED MY REPUTATION AS A "GOURMET COOK." I ALSO RECALL THE DELICATELY LIGHT QUENELLES THAT COULD HAVE DOUBLED AS GOLF BALLS. TAKE MY ADVICE: EXPERIMENTING WITH NEW RECIPES IS FINE, BUT NOT WHEN YOU'RE INVITING IMPORTANT GUESTS FOR DINNER.

DUST OFF THE PRECIOUS CHINA, SILVER, AND CRYSTAL FOR THIS DINNER. COVER THE TABLE WITH THAT HAND-EMBROIDERED TABLECLOTH YOU THOUGHT YOU'D NEVER USE. CREATE AN INTIMATE, GLOWING TABLE WITH SILVER CANDLESTICKS AND WHITE FLOWERS. CARVE THE LAMB AT THE TABLE, SERVE THE SPINACH AND POTATOES FROM SILVER VEGETABLE DISHES, AND USE A DECORATIVE UNDERLINER FOR YOUR DESSERT PLATES. OPEN THE WINE, TURN ON SOFT MUSIC, AND WELCOME YOUR GUESTS.

Autumn Root Vegetable Bisque

THE RICH, SUBTLE FLAVOR OF THIS VEGETABLE BISQUE REPLETE WITH BACON, GARLIC, GINGER, AND PUMPKIN SETS THE TONE FOR AN ELEGANT DINING EXPERIENCE.

KITCHENWARE: chef's knife, vegetable peeler, pepper mill, large saucepan

PREPARATION TIME: 30 minutes

COOKING TIME: 40 minutes

4 STRIPS SMOKED BACON, FINELY DICED

2 LEEKS, CUT INTO $^1/_8$-INCH-THICK ROUNDS

1 CLOVE GARLIC, FINELY MINCED

7 CUPS CHICKEN BROTH (FRESH OR CANNED, UNSALTED)

$^1/_4$ TEASPOON FINELY MINCED FRESH GINGER

$^1/_4$ TEASPOON GROUND ALLSPICE

FRESHLY GROUND PEPPER

1 $^1/_2$ CUPS UNSWEETENED PUMPKIN PUREE

1 TEASPOON SUGAR

2 PEARS, PEELED, CORED, AND DICED

1 LARGE CARROT, PEELED AND CUT INTO $^1/_8$-INCH DICE (ABOUT $^1/_2$ CUP)

1 SMALL TURNIP, PEELED AND CUT INTO $^1/_8$-INCH DICE (ABOUT $^1/_2$ CUP)

GARNISH:

$^1/_2$ CUP CRÈME FRAÎCHE (AVAILABLE IN THE DAIRY DEPARTMENT OF GOURMET FOOD STORES) OR SOUR CREAM

1. Cook the bacon in its own fat in the saucepan. Sauté the leeks in the bacon fat for 8 minutes. Add the garlic and cook for 1 minute more over low heat.

2. Add the chicken broth, ginger, allspice, pepper, pumpkin, sugar, and pears. Bring the soup to a boil and simmer for 15 minutes. Add the carrot and turnip and simmer for about 15 minutes more, until the vegetables are just tender.

SERVICE: Ladle the bisque into pretty soup bowls and garnish with the crème fraîche or sour cream. Make sure each serving has plenty of vegetables.

COOK'S TIP: The pumpkin puree makes the soup thick. If it is too thick, add more chicken broth and reseason.

Rosemary-Roasted Rack of Lamb with Cabernet Wine Sauce

RACK OF LAMB IS A "SPECIAL OCCASION" FOOD. IT'S NOT DIFFICULT TO COOK, YET IT

RANKS WITH ENTRÉES PREPARED BY A FOUR-STAR CHEF.

KITCHENWARE: chef's knife, pepper mill, food processor, small mixing bowl, baking pan, instant meat thermometer

PREPARATION TIME: 20 minutes (not including Cabernet Wine Sauce)

ROASTING TIME: 30 minutes

TWO 7-RIB RACKS OF LAMB, CLEANED AND TRIMMED (ASK THE BUTCHER TO REMOVE THE BACKBONE AND CAP FROM THE RACK OF LAMB AND TO "FRENCH" THE RIBS.)

SALT AND FRESHLY GROUND PEPPER

1 CUP FRESH WHITE BREAD CRUMBS (SEE COOK'S TIPS)

2 TEASPOONS FINELY CHOPPED FRESH ROSEMARY

4 CLOVES GARLIC, FINELY MINCED

4 TABLESPOONS (½ STICK) SWEET BUTTER, SOFTENED

1 RECIPE CABERNET WINE SAUCE (RECIPE FOLLOWS)

1. Preheat the oven to 400 degrees.

2. Rub salt and pepper on both sides of the lamb. Mix the bread crumbs with the rosemary, garlic, and butter. Spread the mixture over the top and sides of the racks.

3. Put the lamb in the baking pan and place on the middle rack of the oven. Roast for 25 to 30 minutes, until the instant thermometer reads 125 to 130 degrees and lamb is rosy pink and juicy.

4. While the lamb roasts, prepare the Cabernet Wine Sauce without the drippings.

SERVICE: Allow the lamb to rest for 10 to 15 minutes before carving. The natural juices will settle and drip from the lamb into the baking pan. Reserve these juices for the Cabernet Wine Sauce. Serve 3 rib chops per person, over a pool of Cabernet Wine Sauce.

COOK'S TIPS:

❖ To make bread crumbs, cut the crusts away from day-old bread. Place the bread in the bowl of the food processor and process until you have fine crumbs. Store, covered, in the refrigerator or freezer.

❖ Lamb is perfectly wonderful when pink and juicy. Serve the end chops to those who prefer their lamb better done.

❖ Cabernet Wine Sauce is also excellent served with "New York Steak House" Fillet of Beef (page 142).

CABERNET WINE SAUCE

KITCHENWARE: chef's knife, large sauté pan

PREPARATION TIME: 5 minutes

COOKING TIME: 8 minutes

3 TABLESPOONS SWEET BUTTER	$\frac{1}{2}$ TEASPOON DIJON MUSTARD
2 SHALLOTS, FINELY CHOPPED	DRIPPINGS FROM THE ROASTED LAMB
1 CUP CABERNET WINE	
1$\frac{1}{2}$ CUPS BEEF BROTH (FRESH OR CANNED, UNSALTED)	

1. Heat 2 tablespoons of the butter in the sauté pan. Add the shallots and cook until soft, 2 to 3 minutes.

2. Add the wine and reduce over high heat for 2 minutes. Stir in the beef broth and mustard over high heat. Swirl in the remaining tablespoon of butter and add the pan drippings from the lamb.

MAKES 1 CUP

New Potatoes with Balsamic Vinegar Glaze

BALSAMIC VINEGAR INFUSED IN THE GLAZE OF THE NEW POTATOES LENDS A CRISP TASTE AND A FINE CONTRAST TO THE SEASONINGS ON THE LAMB.

KITCHENWARE: chef's knife, pepper mill, small saucepan, baking pan, pastry brush

PREPARATION TIME: 15 minutes

COOKING TIME: 25 minutes

4 TABLESPOONS (½ STICK) SWEET BUTTER

2 LARGE SHALLOTS, FINELY CHOPPED

¼ CUP BALSAMIC VINEGAR

SALT AND FRESHLY GROUND PEPPER

2 TABLESPOONS FINELY CHOPPED FRESH FLAT-LEAF PARSLEY

15 MEDIUM NEW POTATOES, SCRUBBED CLEAN AND QUARTERED

1. Preheat the oven to 450 degrees.

2. Heat the butter in the small saucepan. Add the shallots and sauté until soft, 4 to 5 minutes. Add the vinegar, salt and pepper to taste, and 1 tablespoon of the parsley. Cook over high heat for 1 minute.

3. Put the potatoes in the baking pan and coat them well with the butter glaze. Bake for 20 minutes (shake the pan after 10 minutes), until browned. If the potatoes have not browned, put them under the broiler for a few minutes.

   If you put the potatoes under the broiler, watch them carefully to avoid burning.

SERVICE: Coat the potatoes with the remaining tablespoon of parsley and serve with the rack of lamb.

COOK'S TIPS:

❖ The new potatoes work well with any roasted meat, poultry, or grilled fish.

❖ Add diced smoked ham, chunks of leftover pot roast, or roasted lamb for a "hash" supper.

Sautéed Spinach and Leeks

KITCHENWARE: chef's knife, pepper mill, large sauté pan

PREPARATION TIME: 12 minutes

COOKING TIME: 10 minutes

1 TABLESPOON VIRGIN OLIVE OIL

2 TABLESPOONS SWEET BUTTER

2 LARGE LEEKS, WASHED, CUT INTO
1/8-INCH-THICK SLICES (WHITE PART ONLY)

1 POUND FRESH SPINACH, RINSED WELL,
HEAVY STEMS REMOVED

SALT AND FRESHLY GROUND PEPPER

1. Heat the oil and butter in the sauté pan. Add the leeks and sauté over medium heat for 7 to 8 minutes, until soft.

2. Add the spinach. Toss and coat the leaves well with the oil. Cook for 2 to 3 minutes, until the spinach wilts. Season with salt and pepper to taste.

   Do not overcook the spinach; the leaves should be a vibrant green.

SERVICE: Serve the spinach with the rack of lamb and new potatoes.

COOK'S TIP: Sauté plum tomatoes and minced garlic and add to the spinach for variety.

Vanilla Bean Crème Brûlée

A SMOOTH FINISH TO AN ELEGANT DINNER PARTY.

KITCHENWARE: small knife, grater, small heavy-bottomed saucepan, 2 medium mixing bowls, fine-mesh strainer, whisk, four 10-ounce ramekins, large baking pan, baking sheet

PREPARATION TIME: 30 minutes

COOKING TIME: 10 minutes

BAKING TIME: 1 hour

1 1/2 CUPS HALF-AND-HALF	8 1/2 TABLESPOONS SUGAR
1 CUP HEAVY CREAM	5 EGG YOLKS
1 VANILLA BEAN, SPLIT IN HALF LENGTHWISE	1 TEASPOON GRATED ORANGE ZEST
	2 TABLESPOONS GRAND MARNIER LIQUEUR
PINCH OF SALT	

1. Preheat the oven to 350 degrees.

2. In a heavy-bottomed saucepan, heat the half-and-half and heavy cream with the vanilla bean and salt. Bring the liquid to a simmer.

3. While the cream is simmering, whisk 7 tablespoons of the sugar, the egg yolks, and the zest in a mixing bowl, until the ingredients are combined.

4. When the cream begins to simmer, remove it from the heat. Pour a little of the hot mixture into the sugar and eggs, whisking constantly.

    Pouring a little of the hot mixture into the cold tempers the uneven temperatures of the ingredients. Tempering the egg yolks with the hot cream is the tricky step. If all the hot cream is quickly poured directly into the eggs, the eggs will scramble.

    In a steady stream, slowly add the remaining cream to the eggs while whisking. Whisk for 1 minute more to make certain all the sugar dissolves.

5. Put the Grand Marnier into a bowl. Pour the custard through the fine-mesh strainer into the liqueur. Fill the ramekins with the cream.

6. Place the ramekins in the shallow baking pan. Add hot water to the pan until it is halfway up the sides of the ramekins. Bake for 1 hour, or until the custard is just slightly wet in the center.

7. Remove the pan from the oven. Take the ramekins out of the water bath and cool the crème brûlée at room temperature.

    If made early in the day, the custards should be refrigerated at this point. Bring to room temperature before candying the tops.

8. One hour before serving, preheat the broiler. Sprinkle the remaining sugar evenly over the custards. Put the ramekins on a baking sheet 4 inches from the broiler and broil until the sugar turns a caramel color and bubbles, about 30 seconds.

    Watch the crème brûlées carefully. They should caramelize, not burn.

SERVICE: Serve 1 custard per person. We like to serve this dessert with seasonal fresh fruits (strawberries, raspberries, or peaches). A simple butter cookie (page 165) also adds a nice touch.

COOK'S TIP: Crème brûlée is delightful with coffee, almond, or ginger flavorings. Substitute 2 tablespoons of one of these for the Grand Marnier and orange zest.

Cooking Together
The Dinner Party

SEVERAL DAYS IN ADVANCE

COOK 1: AUTUMN ROOT VEGETABLE BISQUE

Dice the bacon, wash and cut the leeks, mince the garlic and ginger, and dice the carrot and turnip. Cover each with plastic wrap and refrigerate.

SAUTÉED SPINACH AND LEEKS

Wash and cut the leeks and refrigerate, covered.

COOK 2: ROSEMARY-ROASTED RACK OF LAMB

Make the bread crumbs for the lamb. Refrigerate or freeze, covered. Chop the rosemary and mince the garlic, cover each, and refrigerate.

NEW POTATOES WITH BALSAMIC VINEGAR GLAZE

Chop the shallots and the parsley, cover each, and refrigerate.

THE NIGHT BEFORE

COOK 1: AUTUMN ROOT VEGETABLE BISQUE

Make the bisque, cool to room temperature, and refrigerate, covered.

COOK 2: SAUTÉED SPINACH AND LEEKS

Rinse the spinach, remove the stems, and dry well. Refrigerate in a plastic bag, loosely packed.

VANILLA BEAN CRÈME BRÛLÉE

Separate the eggs. Refrigerate the yolks and freeze the whites for another use.

The Morning of the Dinner

COOK 1: **ROSEMARY-ROASTED RACK OF LAMB WITH CABERNET WINE SAUCE**

Prepare the lamb as described in step 2. Put it in the baking pan and refrigerate, uncovered. Prepare the sauce. (You will add the lamb drippings just before serving.)

SAUTÉED SPINACH AND LEEKS

Sauté the leeks and store in a cool place in the kitchen. If your kitchen tends to be hot, refrigerate the leeks right in the sauté pan.

COOK 2: **NEW POTATOES WITH BALSAMIC VINEGAR GLAZE**

Make the glaze for the new potatoes (step 2). Keep the glaze in the saucepan at room temperature.

VANILLA BEAN CRÈME BRÛLÉE

Make the crème brûlée through step 7. Cool to room temperature and refrigerate.

TOGETHER: Peel and quarter the new potatoes. Put them in a large bowl, cover completely with cold water, and refrigerate. Assemble all garnishes.

One Hour Before Dinner

COOK 1: **NEW POTATOES WITH BALSAMIC VINEGAR**

Preheat the oven, dry the potatoes well, and complete the recipe. When the potatoes are finished, place them in a warm spot in the kitchen. (To warm, put them in a 250-degree oven when the lamb has finished roasting.)

AUTUMN ROOT VEGETABLE BISQUE

Reheat the bisque in the top of a stainless-steel double boiler. If the bisque is too thick after heating, add chicken broth to thin, and reseason.

COOK 2: **VANILLA BEAN CRÈME BRÛLÉE**

Bring the ramekins to room temperature and caramelize the tops under the broiler as directed in step 8.

ROSEMARY-ROASTED RACK OF LAMB WITH CABERNET WINE SAUCE

As soon as the potatoes are finished, lower the oven temperature from 450 degrees to 400 degrees and roast the lamb. *The lamb should be timed so that you remove it from the oven just before sitting down to eat.* Add the pan drippings to the Cabernet Wine Sauce.

TOGETHER: Just before dinner, one cook sautés the spinach and leeks while the other carves the lamb. The spinach and leeks can be kept warm over very low heat while the vegetable bisque is served.

Chapter 10

Glossary of Cooking Terms

BAKE: To cook with dry heat.

BASTE: To moisten foods while cooking.

BEAT: To work with a mixture and make smooth or increase the volume with a hand whip or in the bowl of an electric mixer.

BLANCH: To immerse fruits or vegetables in boiling water, then immediately place them in cold water to set their color and texture. (Blanching is often a first cooking step before adding an ingredient to a food that will be cooked again.)

BLEND: To mix ingredients together.

BOIL: To heat a liquid until it bubbles rapidly from the bottom to the top of the pan.

BRAISE: To first brown meat or vegetables in fat, then add a small amount of liquid, cover, and cook slowly on top of the range or in the oven.

BROIL: To cook under direct heat.

BRUSH: To spread a food (such as margarine, butter, or a glaze) using a brush.

CARAMELIZE: To melt sugar slowly over low heat in a heavy-bottom saucepan, stirring constantly until the sugar becomes a caramel-brown liquid.

CHOP: To cut food into smaller pieces using a sharp knife.

COAT: To completely cover foods (with flour, bread crumbs, or ground nuts).

CREAM: To beat a shortening by hand or in the bowl of an electric mixer until light and creamy.

CUBE: To cut foods into $1/2$- to 1-inch squares with a sharp chef's knife.

DICE: To cut foods into pieces smaller than a cube with a sharp chef's knife.

DREDGE: To coat foods in a dry ingredient (such as flour or nuts).

DUST: To sprinkle food lightly with a dry ingredient (such as flour or sugar).

FOLD: To thoroughly combine two ingredients (such as beaten egg whites and cake batter) with an up-and-over motion of the hand.

FRY: To cook a food in a small amount of fat on top of the stove. Deep-frying requires a deep layer of fat into which the food is completely immersed. Both methods produce a golden crisp crust.

GARNISH: To decorate foods with herbs, fruits, nuts, or creams.

GLAZE: To coat foods (such as fruits, cakes, pies, or sweet breads) with a warmed syrup.

GRATE: To rub foods (such as cheese, lemon, or orange peel) over a hand grater and reduce them to varying degrees of fineness.

JULIENNE: To slice foods (such as carrots, zucchini, or peppers) into thin strips the size of matchsticks.

KNEAD: To work dough with the palm of your hand until it becomes elastic.

MARINATE: To cover foods completely with an infused liquid (such as a warm vinaigrette) to add flavor before cooking.

MELT: To warm a solid food (such as butter or margarine) until it becomes liquid.

MINCE: To cut foods finer than a dice using a sharp knife.

MIX: To stir ingredients until they are thoroughly combined.

PARE: To cut away the coverings (such as the peel or skin of fruits or vegetables) with a vegetable peeler or paring knife.

PEEL GARLIC: Separate the cloves of garlic from the head. Place the cloves on a work counter. Press the flat side of a knife against each garlic clove. The skin will split and slip off.

PUREE: To mix foods (such as vegetables, sauces, and soups) in a food processor, blender, or a fine strainer until creamy and smooth.

SAUTÉ: To fry foods (such as garlic, shallots, and onions) on top of the range in a small amount of fat until golden.

SEAR: To brown the surface of foods (such as beef, lamb, or pork) over high heat on top of the range.

SEED A TOMATO: First make sure that the chef's knife is sharp and the tomato is ripe. Cut the tomato crosswise, not through the stem. Hold the tomato over a bowl lined with a fine-mesh strainer and gently squeeze the seeds out. Rinse out any seeds remaining in the tomato. Save the juice for the recipe.

SIFT: To put dry ingredients (such as flour or baking powder) through a fine-mesh strainer or a sifter.

WHIP: To rapidly beat foods (such as egg yolks, egg whites, or cream) with a hand whisk or in the bowl of an electric mixer.

Chapter 11

～

The Well-Stocked Pantry

*T*hink of the Well-Stocked Pantry as a treasure chest overflowing with foods that will save your celebration in a culinary crisis. We certainly hope the mischievous kitchen witch will not decide to haunt your kitchen, but if one shows up, turn to the Well-Stocked Pantry for the answers to your problems. We'll share just a few of our crazed experiences when we were eternally grateful to have a well-stocked pantry. The night our *invited* friends brought their *uninvited* houseguests to our small intimate dinner for eight is an evening we will never forget. We had opted to serve individual fillet mignons and purchased exactly eight portions, since they are "caviar expensive." Now we were serving not eight, but ten. We chose a wonderful pâté from the pantry to solve the beef dilemma. Each fillet mignon was cut in half and heaped generously with pâté. We served a half-fillet mignon to each guest, offered seconds, and enjoyed an unexpected elegant dinner for two with the leftovers.

Then there was the evening we cooked wild rice until it looked and tasted like mush and instinctively knew that adding toasted pecans would not resurrect the crisp, natural grain in the rice. The wild rice mush was remedied with the addition of canned white beans from the pantry. We ground the white beans in the food processor until they were chunky, blended them with the rice, and tossed in the toasted pecans to create a crunchy texture.

Our favorite saga is about the duck we decided to braise instead of roast. We were brave, trying a new recipe on company, something, we must admit, we did often with good results. On this occasion, however, our timer found an inopportune moment to stop ticking. The overcooked bird promptly fell apart, leaving pieces of duck floating in a casserole of broth. Resurrecting the duck took a bit of ingenuity. First we removed the duck meat from the bones and shredded it. The duck broth was then reduced and defatted until the liquid resembled strong brewed tea. Moistening the duck with the strong "tea" gave it a wonderful, gamey flavor. Turning to the pantry, we added chopped water chestnuts and bean sprouts. A combination of soy and hoisin sauces enhanced the flavor. Since the plan was to serve lentils with the braised duck, we added ginger to the lentils, which complemented our new oriental concoction!

These trials and tribulations would have been impossible to solve without a cache of food in the pantry.

The Well-Stocked Pantry is filled with the necessities you must have, not only for your daily cooking, but also to remedy disasters. We have stocked The Epicurean Pantry with foods you will occasionally need when you are cooking dinner for company or when you simply crave something wild and wonderful for yourselves.

The Well-Stocked Pantry

DRIED HERBS AND SPICES

BASIL: GROUND

BAY LEAVES

CARAWAY SEEDS

CHILI POWDER

CHIVES: FREEZE-DRIED

CINNAMON: GROUND AND STICKS

CURRY POWDER

DILLWEED

GARLIC POWDER

GINGER: GROUND AND CRYSTALLIZED

NUTMEG: GROUND

ONION POWDER

OREGANO: GROUND

PAPRIKA

PEPPER: GROUND BLACK, GROUND WHITE, AND CAYENNE

PEPPERCORNS: BLACK

ROSEMARY: GROUND

SAFFRON THREADS

SAGE: GROUND

SALT: TABLE AND KOSHER

TARRAGON: GROUND

THYME: GROUND

DRY STAPLES

BAKING POWDER: DOUBLE ACTING

BAKING SODA

BEANS: CANNED

BEANS: DRIED LENTILS, WHITE, AND RED

BEEF BROTH: UNSALTED CANNED

BOUILLON CUBES: CHICKEN, BEEF, AND VEGETABLE

BREAD CRUMBS: UNSEASONED

CHICKEN BROTH: UNSALTED CANNED

CHOCOLATE: SEMISWEET SQUARES, UNSWEETENED SQUARES, AND SEMISWEET MORSELS

CHOCOLATE WAFERS

COCOA: UNSWEETENED

COFFEE: INSTANT ESPRESSO

CORNSTARCH

CRACKERS: YOUR FAVORITE

CREAM OF TARTAR

DESSERT SAUCES: CHOCOLATE AND BERRY

DRIED FRUITS: RAISINS

FLOUR: UNBLEACHED, ALL-PURPOSE, AND PASTRY

GELATIN: UNFLAVORED POWDERED

GINGERSNAPS

HOISIN SAUCE: CANNED

HONEY

HORSERADISH: WHITE GRATED, JARRED

LEMON JUICE

MAYONNAISE

MILK: SWEETENED CONDENSED AND
EVAPORATED

MUSTARD: DIJON AND WHOLE-GRAIN

NUTS: ALMONDS, PINE NUTS, AND WALNUTS

OILS: VEGETABLE, OLIVE, AND CANOLA

OLIVES: BLACK AND GREEN

PASTA: DRIED FETTUCINI AND PENNE

PEANUT BUTTER

PRESERVES: FRUIT JAMS

RICE: LONG-GRAIN CONVERTED, BROWN, AND
WILD

SOY SAUCE

SUGAR: GRANULATED AND CONFECTIONERS'

TABASCO

TEA: YOUR FAVORITE REGULAR AND HERBAL

TOMATOES: WHOLE PLUM, TOMATO PUREE,
AND PASTE

VANILLA EXTRACT

VINEGARS: WHITE, RED WINE, AND CIDER

WINES: DRY BURGUNDY AND WHITE
CHARDONNAY

YEAST: ACTIVE DRY

The Epicurean Pantry

DRIED HERBS AND SPICES

ALLSPICE: GROUND

CELERY SEED

JUNIPER BERRIES

MINT: GROUND

MUSTARD SEED

PICKLING SPICES

POPPY SEEDS

PUMPKIN SEEDS

SAVORY: GROUND

SESAME SEEDS: BLACK

TURMERIC: GROUND

DRY STAPLES

ANCHOVIES: CANNED

ARTICHOKE HEARTS: CANNED OR JARRED

CANDIED VIOLETS AND PANSIES

CAPERS: JARRED

CHUTNEY: MAJOR GREY'S

DRIED FRUITS: CURRANTS, APRICOTS,
GOLDEN RAISINS, AND CRANBERRIES

EXTRACT: ALMOND, LEMON, AND ORANGE

GARLIC: MINCED IN JARS

GRAINS: COUSCOUS, BARLEY, BASMATI RICE,
AND BULGAR

HONEY MUSTARD

LIQUEURS: COINTREAU, AMARETTO, GRAND
MARNIER, CALVADOS, BRANDY, AND
COGNAC

MUSHROOMS: DRIED SHIITAKE OR PORCINI

OILS: SAFFLOWER, PEANUT, SESAME,
HAZELNUT, AND GARLIC

OLIVES: PITTED BLACK, NIÇOISE, AND
PITTED GREEN

PEPPERCORNS: PINK AND GREEN

PEPPERS: JALAPEÑO, CHIPOLTE, AND CHILI

PESTO: JARRED

PICKLES: CORNICHONS

PRESERVES: RED CURRANT JELLY AND
ORANGE MARMALADE

RED BELL PEPPERS: ROASTED

SUN-DRIED CHERRIES

SUN-DRIED TOMATOES: PACKED IN OIL

VINEGARS: TARRAGON, BALSAMIC, AND
RASPBERRY

WATER CHESTNUTS: CANNED

WINES: MARSALA, SHERRY, MADEIRA, AND
PORT

LEMONS

MILK: SKIM

ONIONS: SPANISH, RED

POTATOES: IDAHO AND RED BLISS

SOUR CREAM

TOMATOES

YOGURT: PLAIN

FROZEN FOODS

BEEF: GROUND

CHICKEN BREASTS: BONELESS

ICE CREAM: YOUR FAVORITE

PASTAS: RAVIOLI AND TORTELLINI

PHYLLO DOUGH

POUND CAKE

PUFF PASTRY

RASPBERRIES

SORBET: YOUR FAVORITE

SPINACH: CHOPPED

PRACTICAL PERISHABLE STAPLES

BUTTER: SWEET

CHEESE: CREAM, CHEDDAR, AND PARMESAN

COTTAGE CHEESE

EGGS: WHOLE LARGE

GARLIC: FRESH

HALF-AND-HALF

Chapter 12

~

Registry Planner

Cookware

8-inch nonstick skillet (medium)

12-inch nonstick skillet (large)

1-quart nonstick saucepan (small)

3-quart nonstick saucepan (medium)

5-quart nonstick saucepan (large)

$1\frac{1}{2}$-quart nonstick sauté pan (small)

5-quart nonstick sauté pan (medium)

8-quart stockpot

5-quart stir-fry pan

Large nonstick roaster

Stainless-steel double boiler

Bakeware

6-cup nonstick muffin tin

12-cup nonstick muffin tin

24-cup nonstick mini-muffin tin

Nonstick loaf pan

2 nonstick baking sheets

2 nonstick baking pans

Two 9-inch round nonstick cake pans

9-inch nonstick springform pan

Quiche pan

Set of 3 mixing bowls

Ramekins

Tapered rolling pin

Cooling rack

Measuring cups

Measuring spoons

1-quart liquid measure

Flour sifter

Strainers, assorted sizes

Knives

$3\frac{1}{2}$-inch paring knife

$4\frac{1}{2}$-inch paring knife

8-inch carving knife

10-inch slicer

Chef's knife

Bread knife

Sharpening steel

Knife box

Set of steak knives

Small Appliances

Tea kettle

4-cup coffeemaker

12-cup coffeemaker

Coffee grinder

Juicer

Waffle iron

4-slice toaster

Food processor (with grater and shredder)

ELECTRIC MIXER (WHISK, BEATER, DOUGH
HOOK ATTACHMENTS)

ELECTRIC CAN OPENER

FOOD MILL

ACCESSORIES

COLANDER

WOK

FONDUE SET

PEPPER MILL

SALT SHAKER (OR MILL)

CARVING BOARD

WOODEN SPOONS, ASSORTED SIZES

SPATULA (RUBBER AND METAL)

MEAT FORK

SLOTTED SPOON

SOUP LADLE

BULB BASTER

WHISKS

GARLIC PRESS

VEGETABLE PEELER

CORER

TIMER

INSTANT MEAT THERMOMETER

DEEP-FRYING THERMOMETER

CAKE TESTER

SALAD SPINNER

KITCHEN SHEARS

BARBECUE SET

PASTRY BAG

COOKIE CUTTERS

ZESTER

DISH TOWELS

HIS AND HERS APRONS

4 OVEN MITTS

4 POTHOLDERS

SET OF STORAGE BOWLS (FOR FREEZER
AND/OR REFRIGERATOR)

Index